the Gift of Fire

edited by
Ian Macpherson

Dimension Books
Bethany Fellowship, Inc.
Minneapolis, Minnesota

PREFACE

"Only the preacher proceeds still upon the idea that folk come to church desperately anxious to discover what happened to the Jebusites."

The man who said that was no cynical critic of the contemporary pulpit; he was himself one of the foremost spiritual spokesmen of the twentieth century.

He knew what he was saying; and what indictment of preaching could be more utterly devastating than this charge which he brings against it—that of irrelevance?

Yet who will deny that many modern ministers lay themselves wide open to it? They handle the Bible as if it were a Dodo's egg, and not, as it is, an atomic bomb. Such preachers give the impression that only an archaeologist or an antiquarian could have a deep interest in the Holy Book. To convey such an impression is fatal, and undoubtedly one of the reasons why often so few are to be found in the pews.

For the preacher of today an extremely pressing problem is that of imparting to his message a perceptible pertinence to our age.

How can this be done?

One obvious way is to deal in his sermons with the urgent issues of the hour.

Another is to start with "life-situations"—to begin with some individual human problem.

While there may be much merit in both procedures, the real answer lies elsewhere.

To be relevant, preaching must be Spirit-inspired.

Nor must we stop with an analysis of the needs of ordained ministers. Every Christian has upon him the weighty responsibility of "preaching," face to face, person to person, and day by day. And the individual witness must be every bit as relevant as the Sunday morning sermon. To be relevant, witnessing also must be inspired.

Because each of the contributors to this brief book believes this—despite widely differing views on aspects of the subject—the editor has compiled this short symposium.

The little volume is not at all "planned." No effort has been made to dictate to the writers. Each has been given a completely free hand. At times their comments overlap, but that only serves to underline the more important truths concerning the Spirit of God.

These concise and practical writings all revolve around one theme—the Pentecostal gift of the Holy Spirit. They are offered to every concerned Christian to help lift him to a place of liberated life and witness for Christ.

CONTENTS

THE PROMISE
Charles J. Clarke

Wait for the promise of the Father.

Acts 1:4

Our text is taken from Luke's account of a crucial scene in the New Testament drama. The risen Christ is giving to His disciples their final briefing. These eleven men, chosen by our Lord "to be with him that he might send them forth," had passed through the wonderful years of His earthly ministry; had been broken by the terrible ordeal of the Crucifixion and had emerged into the unbelievable experience of the resurrection appearances, until at last they knew they had an ever-living Lord who was now teaching them their apostolic role in the kingdom of God—that supernatural realm which had been manifested in Jesus and which was presently to be extended by them. "But wait," said their risen Lord, "wait at Jerusalem for the promise of the Father about which I have told you."

Let us study the New Testament to see what this promise is, whether it was fulfilled in the experience of the apostles and whether it is a promise extended to us.

Jesus Promises the Holy Spirit

The promise of the Father was that the apostles should be baptized in the Holy Spirit;

for in the verses following our text Jesus goes on to say: "John baptized in water, but before many days you shall be baptized in the Holy Spirit" (Acts 1:5).

When had the apostles been told of this promise? For the answer we must turn to John 14, 15 and 16, to the scene in the Upper Room on the eve of the arrest of Jesus in the Garden of Gethsemane. The vital teaching about the promise begins in John 13:31 after Judas had left the supper table and gone out into the night. Then Jesus began to speak to His eleven apostles. "I am going to leave you," He said, "I am going back to My Father. But I will not leave you bereft. I shall send you another Leader, the Paraclete, who will guide you into all truth. I am with you, but He shall be in you. I am about to leave you, but He will be with you for ever. He is the Spirit of My Father who works through Me. He is My Spirit and He will work through you. He will create within you a mystical union with the Father and with Me. In that day you will know that I am in My Father and you in Me and I in you (John 14:20). In that day you will have a power in prayer you have not known before (John 15:23). In that day you will have power in service you have never known before, for the works that I do you shall do also" (John 14:12).

In effect Jesus told them that they should be possessed by His Spirit, the same Spirit of His Father who had worked so powerfully through Him; and that, being so possessed and used, they would be His body through which He would still pursue His messianic and redemptive mission on earth.

Jesus Fulfilled His Promise

On the day of Pentecost the promise was fulfilled. These men obeyed the word of Jesus and waited in Jerusalem until the Spirit came. They waited in prayer with others numbering in all one hundred and twenty, including the mother of Jesus and His closest friends.

As they waited, suddenly a sound like that of a powerful wind was heard coming down until it filled the room. They saw tongues of fire resting upon the head of each disciple. And they were all filled with the Holy Spirit and spoke with other tongues as the Spirit gave them utterance.

The immediate result was astounding. Crowds were drawn to the spot and listened to this outpouring of praise in tongues. Some, from foreign lands, recognized their own languages. Others were puzzled and amazed. Some mocked and said: "They're drunk!" Then Peter got up and explained that they were not drunk. His explanation became an inspired testimony to Jesus until at last he asserted: "Let all the house of Israel know with certainty that God has made this Jesus whom you crucified both Lord and Christ" (Acts 2:36). "Being therefore exalted at the right hand of God, and having received from the Father the promised Holy Spirit, he has poured out this which you see and hear" (Acts 2:33).

Pentecost was like the bursting out of a fountain of spiritual life which flooded the surrounding countryside. This community of Spirit-filled disciples of Jesus multiplied rapidly and spread through the world of the first century. They were an amazing company, as we should expect such God-intoxicated people to be.

They were full of joy. When Paul and Silas

11

were beaten and cast into the inner dungeon of the prison and their feet made fast in stocks: "At midnight they sang praises to God and the prisoners heard them" (Acts 16:25).

They were full of love, even for their enemies. Their first martyr prayed for his murderers as his Lord had done on Calvary.

They were full of power. Signs and wonders occurred wherever they went. When Peter was imprisoned and condemned to death, they prayed into the night until the prison doors opened and Peter walked out. The sick were healed through their ministrations exactly as they had been through the ministry of Jesus.

From the very beginning of their mission they were cruelly opposed. The Jewish authorities killed Stephen by stoning. Herod beheaded James. Saul hauled men and women to prison and to death. In course of time the Roman emperors became alarmed and sought to liquidate them. They threw them to the lions, burnt them at the stake, beheaded them with the sword; but nothing could stop the victorious spread of the Gospel through their powerful witness. At the end of the second century, Tertullian wrote his *Defense of Christianity* and addressed it to the governors of all the Roman provinces. He claimed that Christians were to be found in each stratum of empire life and could not be destroyed in spite of the most cruel persecution. "The blood of the martyrs," said Tertullian, "is the seed of the Church."

So wonderfully had Jesus fulfilled His promise. The Christian community, rapidly spreading through the vast Roman Empire, was confidently aware of its unseen Leadership. Jesus had been with His first disciples in Palestine: His glorious Spirit was now *in* their successors. And they were so very conscious of His indwelling presence. "Greater is he that is in you," wrote the apostle John, "than he who is in the world" (I John 4:3).

The Promise Is To You

When Peter spoke to the crowd at Pentecost, the Holy Spirit so empowered his words that the people were convicted of the sin of Christ-rejection so deeply that they cried out: "What shall we do?" Peter told them what to do, and said that if they followed his instructions "you shall receive the Holy Spirit, for the promise is unto you" (Acts 2:38, 39).

This is a word for us today. The promise is unto us. In these days of political peril, of moral degradation, of impotent religion, this promise is to us. *We* may receive power when the Holy Spirit comes upon us. We too may be baptized in the Holy Spirit. The joy, the peace, the love and the power of the Spirit are promised to us.

Let me give you two illustrations which prove that this promise of Jesus is for our age also.

Samuel Chadwick was a young Methodist minister sent to a difficult task in the village of Stacksteads, and he soon became disheartened because his ministry was so spiritually powerless. He began to search, in Scripture and through prayer, for the answer. He says: "Twelve of us began to pray in band and the answer came. He led us to Pentecost and when it came I could not explain what happened, but I was aware of things unspeakable and full of glory. Some results were immediate. There came into my soul a deep peace, a thrilling joy and a new sense of power. My mind was quickened. I felt I had received a new faculty of understanding. Every power was vitalized. There was a new sense of spring and vitality, a new power of endurance, and a strong man's exhilaration

13

in big things. Things began to happen. What we had endeavoured to do by strenuous activity now came to pass without labour. The same Spirit gave me a new understanding and experience of prayer, and with these gifts came a new endowment of wisdom and power. From the first day of my Pentecost I became a seeker and winner of souls."—*The Path of Pentecost* (London: Hodder & Stoughton)

The second illustration is from J. Cameron Peddie's book *The Forgotten Talent*. Mr. Peddie is a Church of Scotland minister who, during the war years, became burdened with the conviction that the original healing ministry of the Church ought never to have been lost. He therefore decided to practice a vigil each night between eleven and twelve o'clock in his prayer room, waiting upon God and offering himself, body, soul and spirit, to be used to restore this ministry. After four years of this discipline, God answered in a baptism of the Spirit.

He writes: "What happened might have been expected in the sanctuary, a cathedral or some piece of holy ground. But it happened as I stood at the sink in the kitchen paring potatoes, a knife in one hand and a potato in the other. What my thoughts were I cannot remember, but I have no doubt that being alone I was talking to the Father about the work I wished to do. Whatever thoughts engaged my attention, suddenly I felt myself gripped by a strange benevolent power that filled me with an unspeakable sense of happiness. I seemed to be drawn up out of the body and did not know where I was, 'whether in the body or out of it.' It was the supreme and final bliss. Joy filled my heart and overflowed in tears. Helplessly I cried like a child, the tears pouring from my eyes. All I could say was 'Father, O Father!' These were the only words

I could cry, and they were uttered involuntarily and in spite of myself as I wept. When I thought of the sheer joy of the experience I recalled Psalm 16:11: 'In thy presence is fulness of joy; at thy right hand there are pleasures for evermore.' "

Mr. Peddie goes on to explain in the rest of his book that, thrilling as the experience was, its primary purpose was not his happiness, but ministry—a wonderful ministry of healing by which the Divine Spirit who possessed him flowed through him to heal the sick in body and mind; testifying, as many others can do, that the promise is unto us, even now, in this sophisticated twentieth century.

You need not wistfully look back and think how wonderful it must have been to have lived in New Testament days. You are included in the promise now. You may know at this moment a revolutionary, exhilarating penetration of your innermost being by almighty God. Indeed, the promise is your birthright. Jesus died on the cross to procure this inheritance for you. You must not miss it! The promise is unto you.

How You May Receive the Promise

If, even now, you are conscious of a quenchless thirst for this living water, how can you be filled? Here are three key words to lead you into blessing:

(1) *Seek*. Jesus made great promises to seekers. He said that they would find. He told the story of a man who went seeking goodly pearls and said he found the pearl of great price. This is your parable. Seek for the baptism in the Holy Spirit, and you will find. (a) Seek in the Scriptures. Be like the Christians of Berea who "searched the scriptures daily to see if these

things were so" (Acts 17:11). Read carefully through the New Testament and underline every reference to the Holy Spirit. Brood and pray over what you read, and the Holy Spirit will excitingly light up the truth. (b) Seek also in prayer. Underscore that little word *ask* in Luke 11:13. Then put the little word into action. Look at the word *importunity* in Luke 11:8, and see the need to persist in asking. Ask, and ask, and ask in the spirit of wrestling Jacob: "I will not let you go unless you bless me" (Gen. 32:26).

(2) *Yield*. The purpose of the baptism in the Holy Spirit is that you shall become possessed by the Spirit. This is not possible unless you yield your will to Him. Often hindrance to the blessing lies just here—our unwillingness to be possessed, our innate basic disobedience to our divine Lord. As we seek by Bible study and prayer, we become very conscious of being involved in a transaction with the Holy Spirit. He makes quite clear just where our resistance is centered and where He requires obedience. It is here we must yield, opening the gate of the citadel of our being for Him to enter and possess and rule.

(3) *Receive*. There comes a point of our quest where the whole issue is clear. Illumination floods our being. Jesus the Baptizer stands ready to pour into us His own Spirit. He waits for us to say "Yes." Faith is no longer difficult; it is simply the glad response of our whole being to this mighty Lover. In a moment of ecstatic consent we open our hearts wide and find ourselves filled with glory and with God.

Take these three steps, my friend. Claim your inheritance!

THE ISLE AND THE SPIRIT
G. N. M. Collins

I was in the isle that is called Patmos, for the word of God, and for the testimony of Jesus Christ. I was in the Spirit on the Lord's day.
Revelation 1:9, 10

It is deeply suggestive to place side by side two phrases from the Book of Revelation: "I was in the isle. I was in the Spirit."

John was an exile in Patmos because of his faithfulness to the Word of God and the testimony of Jesus. Patmos is less than twelve miles from north to south and some six miles broad at its widest part. In his sea-girt prison John was "cabined, cribbed, and confined"; but, because he was in the Spirit, his soul had wings. Under the inspiration and the guidance of the Holy Spirit, he had such visions of the glory of the risen Lord and such visions of His far-stretching kingdom and its ultimate triumph as have never come our way. Yet we too, in our measure, may get glimpses of these glories and these wonders, and what a difference that ought to make in our lives!

Being in the Spirit Ought to Deliver Us from a Sense of Loneliness

John must have felt lonely enough sometimes in Patmos, with loved ones far away, with no

Christian brother near him to strengthen his hand in God. We can imagine him standing sometimes on the eastern shore of Patmos, gazing wistfully across the sea in the direction of Ephesus where he had labored for Christ so long. He thought perhaps, on this memorable Lord's Day, of the little companies of Christians gathering for worship in Ephesus and the surrounding district. Between him and them many miles of sea rolled, and he must have felt lonely.

In our English language we have the word 'isolation,' which comes through the Italian language from the Latin word for 'island.' That word is needed because a sense of loneliness comes at some time or other to every man and woman. A sense of isolation may overwhelm us far more poignantly in the heart of a vast crowd than in the uninhabited desert. Life for many people is a very lonely affair.

"Nothing is more solemn," wrote Alexander Maclaren, "than that awful loneliness in which each soul of man lives. We stretch out our hands and grasp live hands: yet there is a universe between the two that are nearest and most truly one."

But now, look at John again. Was he really lonely? He has not written many words when he breaks into song: "Unto him that loved us, *loves* us." He who knows that he is "loved with everlasting love," because he has been "led by grace that love to know," having been told this by "the Spirit breathing from above," knows that, as somebody has put it, Christ did not "wait to love him till this late, lonely moment which we call life."

Yet how inspiring it must have been for John to remember that the love of Christ was a present reality! "My Saviour loves me," he may

18

have said to himself. "My Saviour loves me here and now in my sea-girt prison, in my dreariest hours."

When a man is led to sing about the love of God for him, his feeling of loneliness begins to vanish. Though he may have very few friends on earth and though he may sometimes be sadly misunderstood by the friends he has, he knows now that there is One who loves him with a love which many waters cannot quench and which the floods cannot drown.

Was John really lonely? He was cut off from happy fellowship with all his earthly friends, but he was in touch with the shining company of the redeemed in the realms of light and glory, the "great multitude that no man can number," and he was listening to them as they sang the praises of the Lamb. Surely, the man who was in touch with that shining company and who was listening to the music of heaven had gotten rid of the numbing sense of loneliness.

All believers are come, here and now, to "an innumerable company of angels, to the general assembly and church of the firstborn which are written in heaven, and to the spirits of just men made perfect, and to Jesus" (Heb. 12:22-24).

Being in the Spirit Ought to Deliver Us from a Sense of Monotony

It may be taken that John had been condemned to hard labor in the quarries of Patmos; and, if so, it would have meant for him, under the lash of the taskmaster, poor food and insufficient clothing and exposure to the rigor of all kinds of weather. He would have to endure the daily grind of unvarying toil, with no relaxation, for the Lord's Day would not have been a holiday for the quarries of Patmos.

Monotony must have threatened to eat into John's soul, with the sigh and the sob of the sea around the rocky coasts of Patmos forever sounding in his ears.

John might have been expected to succumb to the deadening influences of monotony. But he was in the Spirit, and the Spirit led him to a deeper intensity of soul-experience. Always there was the same hard, grinding toil from one end of the week to the other, but no doubt the risen Lord said to him what He said to one of the churches of Asia: "I know thee where thou dwellest." Always there was the same song of the sea, day after day, but John was listening to the voice that is as the sound of many waters. Always there was the same sun setting in a blaze of glory on the western horizon, but John was in the land where his sun would no more go down; he was gazing on the sea of glass mingled with fire, at the place where

The Lamb with His fair company
Doth on Mount Zion stand.

"Are you not tired of looking at the same scene?" somebody asked a fine old Christian who, during a protracted illness, used to sit through many hours of the long day at the window of his room; and he replied: "I never see the same scene." He was always seeing new wonders in God's fair world. Read the Book of Revelation and note how often John writes: "I saw."

For example, he saw the Throne of God, with the rainbow round about it. To see the Throne of God—always awe-inspiring but always with the rainbow about it, which speaks of the covenant of peace—ought surely, in

20

the words of Ebenezer Erskine, to lift "our heads out of time into eternity," and it ought to mean escape from the monotony which so often keeps us earthbound.

Again, John saw the Lamb in the midst of the Throne, redeeming Love at the heart of the universe, with all the forces of the cosmos bowed in adoration before it.

It is when men have no vision of that love which is at the heart of things that they think of life as dull and monotonous and meaningless.

One of our poets says that "most men in a brazen prison lie," with no vision beyond the walls of their cells, seeing no worthwhile meaning in their daily tasks; and then, too often, they fall asleep in their dreary jails, "unfreed, having seen nothing, still unblessed."

"Having seen nothing." What an epitaph to write over a man's life! "Open my eyes that I may see"—that is a prayer that we may well offer every day, for the measure in which we escape from the sense of the monotony of life is the measure in which we see what John saw.

Being in the Spirit Ought to Deliver us from Narrowness

In our English language we have a word 'insular' which is derived from the Latin word for 'island.' The dictionary says that it means 'belonging to an island,' but that it has also the meaning of 'narrow' or 'prejudiced.'

The people who live on islands are not always narrow-minded, but there are islands of narrowness and prejudice on which some people seem to spend the whole of their lives. They never see very far beyond the village pump; they think "the rustic cackle of their bourg the murmur of the world"; they are the people and wisdom will die with them.

There had been a time when John had been in danger of having his spiritual life sadly spoiled by racial prejudice. He would not have been sorry if fire from heaven had burned up a certain village of the Samaritans. In after years we find John, along with Peter, preaching the Word of God to Samaria, perhaps offering to that same village things from heaven very different from devouring fire! Christian Jews *must* have dealings with Samaritans and, over-leaping age-long barriers, bring to them the Gospel, which is meant for all nations.

In Patmos John sees all racial barriers swept away forever, when the great multitude from all nations and kindreds and people and tongues has been brought into one vast kingdom of God.

We are delivered from all narrowness of outlook when we get a glimpse of the mighty sweep of the purpose of God, and when we remember that He is working that purpose out as year succeeds to year, and that the final triumph of that purpose is assured.

THE PLACE OF POWER
George H. Forester

And Jesus returned in the power of the Spirit to Galilee.

Luke 4:14

Four things are necessary before the Christian can move in the power of the Spirit. These four things were vital even for the Son of God, and they are therefore absolutely indispensable to us. At the present time there are many disappointed Christians, whose disappointment springs from the fact that they thought that, by receiving the baptism with the Holy Spirit, they would be transformed overnight into men and women of tremendous spiritual power. They soon discovered that the baptism with the Spirit, although it undoubtedly enriched their experience of the Lord Jesus, did not bring about the transformation from powerlessness to power which they expected. One has known not a few believers (including some ministers) who have become disillusioned and even resentful against God as a result.

The baptism with the Spirit is a gateway and not a goal. Its Old Testament type is the crossing of the Jordan. This gave Israel a bridgehead in the Land of Promise, but not the possession of the whole land. There were enemies to contest every advance, and immediately after the crossing of the Jordan there was the challenge of Jericho!

It is encouraging to remind ourselves that "all things work together for good to them that love God, to them that are the called according to his purpose" (Rom. 8:28). Among the "all things" are even our failures and disappointments, which can be the means of bringing us to our knees again with renewed determination to seek after God. The Scripture goes on to say: "For whom he did foreknow, he also did predestinate to be conformed to the image of his Son, that he might be the firstborn among many brethren" (Rom. 8:28f.).

Our Lord Jesus trod a certain pathway to bring Him to that dramatic moment described in our text, namely, to His entry into Galilee *in the power of the Spirit*. It did not happen in a flash! There was a sequence of experiences and also a patient waiting for God's time. It was not the descent of the Spirit *alone* that made it possible for Jesus to move in the power of the Spirit. We need to "consider the Apostle and High-priest of our profession" in this matter most carefully, realizing that we must be conformed to His image. If He had to tread a certain road into the power realm, then we must tread the same road. We shall not find a short-cut! The disciple is not above his Master!

Assuming that we are interested in seeing the Church restored to her first-century place of power, let us consider what Scripture reveals as having transpired between the moment when the Lord was baptized in the Jordan and the moment described in our text.

First, the Anointing

It is absolutely clear that the initial step in our Lord's pathway to a ministry of demonstration of the Spirit and of power was that

24

He had to be anointed with the Holy Spirit. We must make a vital distinction between the *indwelling of the Spirit* and the *anointing* of the Spirit *coming upon* the person concerned.

The Lord Jesus surely enjoyed the *indwelling* of the Spirit in fulness from His mother's womb. This was true of John the Baptist, and it is inconceivable that it was not so with the Son of God. The fruit of the Spirit is, in any case, the proof of the indwelling of the Spirit, and was increasingly evident in the Saviour's life, for He "increased in wisdom and in stature, and in favour with God and man" (Luke 2:52).

All the same, it was not the indwelling of the Spirit which caused Jesus to be "a man approved of God by miracles and wonders and signs, which God did by him" (Acts 2:22). This was the result of the Spirit of God *descending* and *remaining* upon Him, so that He could afterwards testify: "The Spirit of the Lord is *upon* me, for he hath *anointed* me" (Luke 4:18). The remainder of the verse paints a vivid picture of the ministry of the One mighty in word and deed.

All true believers know the indwelling of the Holy Spirit as Comforter, Teacher, Sanctifier, Life-giver. "If any man have not the Spirit of Christ, he is none of his" (Rom. 8:9). This is not, however, the whole of a Christian's experience of the Holy Spirit. We should be conformed to the image of God's Son, and know also the anointing of the Holy Spirit coming upon us to equip us for our specific function in the Body of Christ. In the experience of regeneration the blessings of Calvary and the resurrection are personally received, so that the believer walks in newness of life by the Spirit. In the baptism with the Holy Spirit, the blessings of the Day of Pentecost are personally received, so that the believer may share something of the anointing of Christ, who is the Head of the Body. Every Christian should seek a personal Pentecost in the baptism with the Spirit. If Christ needed an anointing, so do we!

Next, the Temptations

The anointing brought our glorious Lord straightway into bitter conflict with the devil, just as the crossing of the Jordan into the Promised Land brought Joshua face to face with Jericho. Satan will always contest a forward move in the working out of God's eternal purpose; and, when the devil saw that Jesus of Nazareth had been anointed with the Holy Ghost and power, he had to launch his counter-attack. His only hope was to try to find something of flesh, self or presumption in the Son of God. The slightest disobedience would have short-circuited God's program for Galilee, for He gives His Spirit "to them that obey him" (Acts 5:32). Though Jesus was the Son of God, "yet learned he obedience by the things which he suffered" (Heb. 5:8). Temptations are the raw materials whereby faith is tried (James 1:2f.) and the obedience of faith proved (I Pet. 1:6f.). Obedience must be *learned.* Jesus had to learn it, and so must we, if we would know the power of the Spirit! The temptations were a vital part in our Master's pathway to the place of power. He emerged from the wilderness as one with complete mastery over the flesh, as one who manifested nothing of self, and as that "Just One" who lived by faith but never by presumption.

Satan's first bid was to exploit the weakness of human flesh. For forty days and forty nights

26

hunger had been sublimated; but, when the days were ended, hunger returned. The flesh began to press its demands. Satan was quick to take advantage of the hunger pangs. Using the perfectly legitimate demands of a hungry body, Satan tried to seduce Christ into obeying his voice. Jesus was set on obeying only the Father's commands. He lived by every Word of God.

The appetites of the flesh can be an instrument in Satan's subtlety, whereby he lures us from taking our orders from God and from God alone. "The flesh lusteth against the Spirit, and the Spirit against the flesh" (Gal. 5:17). The flesh is weak, and if we allow the flesh to dictate to us, we are wide open to the voice of Satan.

We are exhorted to "mortify the deeds of the body" (Rom. 8:13), not in our own strength, but by the Spirit. Paul tells us that he "buffeted" his body and kept it "in subjection" (I Cor. 9:27). By contrast, we live in an age of easy-going self-indulgence in which it is customary to pamper the flesh on an unprecedented scale. Christians unconsciously imbibe the spirit of the age and sermons on mortifying the flesh are not popular in pew or pulpit. Christians today are ruled by the flesh to the extent that they cannot even attend the House of God unless transported by car!

When we begin to share the Master's secret and to esteem every Word of God as of infinitely greater importance than the physical requirements of the flesh, we shall see more power of the Spirit. God will not give His mighty power to a man who has not mastered the flesh!

The second thrust of Satan, as we see again in Luke 4, was the vain endeavor to discover something of self or pride in Jesus. Self-worship is but a step from devil-worship. Satan knew that Jesus looked for a day when the kingdoms of the world would be His, but how seriously the devil misunderstood Christ's motive in this desire! Jesus sought only His Father's glory— not His own! His longing for all to be put in subjection under His own feet was only that He might surrender all to His Father, "that God might be all in all" (I Cor. 15:28). Jesus neither spoke nor acted of Himself (John 5:19; 17:8). There was nothing of self-regard or pride in Him.

It is possible to fast and subdue the flesh for the wrong reason. The Pharisee who stood and prayed reciting his accomplishments (including fasting and tithing!) was far from dead to self! Paul says not only, "I am [or have been] crucified with Christ" (Gal. 2:20), referring to that once-for-all death-blow given to the "old man" at conversion, but he also says, "I die *daily*" (I Cor. 15:31).

Jesus said that the cross must be taken up "daily" (Luke 9:23). It has been well said that many Christians are like men who have died but are still running around the graveyard! The "old man" or self-life must not only be crucified but must be "kept" dead. Self must be constantly "reckoned dead indeed" (Rom. 8:11). A continuous death to self is vital for those who seek the power realm. God simply will not give His glory to another. Have we a lack in the power realm because we have not been sufficiently conformed to the image of Him in whom there was nothing of self?

The devil's last bid was to try to move Jesus from the ground of faith to that of presumption. God's pure Word is the only genuine basis for faith. His Word deceitfully handled, twisted, misquoted or half-quoted or added to, is never a basis for faith. Psalm 91 says nothing whatever about provision for protection when casting oneself down from the temple turret! This was the devil's addition. Had Jesus taken this leap, He would have died the pathetic death of a fanatic and His failure would have dishonored the Father.

Those who seek the power realm need to check constantly that the basis for their faith and ministrations is the Word of God. How easy it is to presume and in so doing to tempt the Lord our God! God is sovereign and has the last word in all matters. All are not called to apostleship, nor are all called to be evangelists. A man needs to abide in his calling. Moreover, we inherit promises by faith and patience and not by rushing ahead of God. "Thou shalt not tempt the Lord thy God" (Luke 4:12).

Further, God's Appointed Hour

At Cana, shortly after the wilderness experience, Jesus said to His mother, "Mine hour is not yet come" (John 2:4). There was a period between His anointing at Jordan and His entry into Gailiee when Jesus moved mainly in Judea and Jerusalem. There were miracles during this period of waiting, but they were not so prolific (only one is described) and not so essential a feature as in the Galilean ministry. This was a time of waiting for God's hour for Galilee. John's first three chapters cover this period, the key to which is the statement in 3:24: "For John was not yet cast into prison."

Of that period Jesus said, "Mine hour is not yet come." Contrast that with Mark 1:14: "Now after that John was put in prison, Jesus came into Galilee, saying, The time is fulfilled." This was the moment when Jesus returned in the power of the Spirit into Galilee. Jesus was waiting for the signal of John's imprisonment. "Now when Jesus had *heard* that John was cast into prison, he departed into Galilee" (Matt. 4:12). Timing is important. "The law and the prophets were until John" (Luke 16:16). Whilst the preparation was incomplete, Galilee had to wait.

Paul was converted on the way to Damascus, baptized with water and with the Spirit three days later, went into Arabia and received wonderful revelations, but he still had to tarry. It was about ten years afterwards that, as the Church fasted and prayed at Antioch, the Holy Spirit said: "Separate me Barnabas and Saul for the work whereunto I have called them" (Acts 13:2). Paul had a ministry before this moment, but we do not read of mighty works in evidence in his ministry until after this moment. Thereafter his ministry assumed a new character. It was "with mighty signs and wonders, by the power of the Spirit of God" (Rom. 15:19).

If Jesus had to wait until God's time was fulfilled; if Paul had to wait at least ten years after he was baptized with the Holy Spirit for this kind of ministry in the power of the Spirit, who are we to think that we can rush straight in? "Fools rush in where angels fear to tread!"

Finally, God's Place

How the name of God's appointed place rings through Scripture where the ministry of Christ is concerned! Galilee! Galilee! Galilee! "Jesus returned in the power of the Spirit into Galilee." Peter said: "That word, I say, ye know, which was published throughout all Judea, and began in Galilee" (Acts 10:37). God had His own *place* as well as His own *time* for Christ to begin His ministry. It had to begin from Galilee!

Galilee speaks of two aspects of a believer's

situation. God has His own place geographically for us to move in in the power of the Spirit. For Jesus it was Galilee, for Paul it was Antioch, for Philip it was Samaria. Are we hindering God because we are in the wrong place?

It also speaks of the all-important matter of our setting in the Body of Christ. I Corinthians 12:28 says, "God hath *set*." Unfortunately, today, many have set themselves, and there is a world of difference between what we consider ourselves to be in the Body of Christ and what God wishes us to be. As certainly as God has a definite place on the map for each one of us to fit into His purpose, He also has a specific function in the Body of Christ for every member of the Body. The Church is rendered less powerful than she might be when members of the Body adopt a hit-and-miss attitude and have never seriously sought the face of the Lord to know their proper function in the Body of Christ. It is vital to be in the right place and performing the right ministry if we would know the power of the Spirit.

There *is* a power realm. Jesus entered into it and He shows us the way. Indeed, He *is* the way! Hallelujah! Peter, Paul, Ananias, Stephen and Philip entered into it in their day. Many have entered into it and are entering into it in this twentieth century. If we would seek the anointing of the Holy Ghost; if we would rejoice in temptations, seeking by the grace and power of God to subdue the flesh, crucify self and learn to walk humbly with our God; if we would patiently wait upon God until His hour for us has struck; and if we would seek to be certain that we are in the right place geographically and in the Body of Christ, we may confidently expect the fulfillment of the promise: "Ye shall receive power after that the Holy Ghost is come upon you" (Acts 1:8).

THE AVAILABILITY OF
THE HOLY SPIRIT

R. C. Gillie

Then Peter said unto them, Repent and be baptized every one of you in the name of Jesus Christ unto the remission of sins; and ye shall receive the gift of the Holy Ghost. For to you is the promise, and to your children, and to all that are afar off, even as many as the Lord our God shall call unto him.

Acts 2:38, 39

I wonder if any of my hearers have desired to have been present at the outpouring of the Holy Spirit on the Day of Pentecost. There are scenes in the New Testament which all of us would love to have shared. When our Lord took the children in His arms, when He sat at peace in the friendly home at Bethany, when He came unannounced to His friends on the evening of the Resurrection Day—each of us would give much to have been there. But at this Pentecostal experience? Do many of us, speaking quite honestly, feel that we have missed much by our absence?

Seen from afar, and at first sight, it looks a confused and excited scene and leaves many of us cold. We need insight if we are to feel any stirrings of desire. What were the facts of Pentecost as they are described to us?

Ecstasy was there, joy brimming over, such

as we rarely experience on earth and most of all rarely in a religious gathering. It was joy that demanded expression, joy of satisfaction and expectancy, transfiguring both past and future.

There was a wonderful feeling of fellowship too. The "many tongues" were the sign of it. The curse of Babel was reversed. All understood the common language of the heart. There was a fusing together of strangers and aliens and comrades.

Most marked of all, a sense of new energy pervaded the one hundred and twenty, an experience of power which bred a high confidence and dwarfed difficulties, until they shrank away to an infinitesimal point. There was a remarkable release and expansion of personality, which people often seek in foolish and material ways.

When we set ourselves to see the inwardness of it, I imagine most of us feel a desire to have shared that experience. You know the upleap of heart on a fine spring morning, or the rare moments in life when you feel strength equal to a sudden challenge — that is a faint echo of the ancient experience. Oh yes, it would have been worthwhile to be present!

But, however that may be, let me scrutinize you a little further. As you look back across the centuries, does not the fact of that far-off experience leave you a little cold? You could listen almost unstirred as I read the record of it. Devoutly, sedately, piously, you are willing to commemorate Whit Sunday. But your pulse was not quickened. Why is it so?

First, many feel that this commemoration of the outpouring of the Spirit is somehow different from Christmas or Easter. Those concern the individual; this is more important for the Church and its ordained ministers. It has to do with the inspiration of the few rather than with the enrichment of the many, with preachers rather than with the rank and file of the Church. We have clericalized Whit Sunday. How curiously we tend to limit the great experiences of the soul! How content we are to lose a part of our spiritual heritage!

Second, there is another thought that chills us even more effectually. This wonderful thing did happen in the early church, but it is past. It won't happen again. Pentecost cannot be repeated. What the apostles experienced is denied to us. The observance of Whit Sunday—Holy Spirit Day—is fitting just as the centenary of the birth of a great man is fitting. But its interest is chiefly retrospective. We visit, so to speak, a memorial building, not a power-house.

One of the most impressive sights as one nears Rome from the south is the long lines of ancient aqueducts, borne upon successive arches across the Campagna. One's eye is immediately attracted and one's imagination stirred. In the channel borne high above these arches, a stream of pure water used to flow from the springs in the lonely hills to the homes of the crowded city. It was a colossal achievement to build these arches, and for years the water flowed above them unfailingly. But now they are just a memorial, rather a pathetic memorial, of a past achievement. Some of the arches are broken, some have vanished, where the channel exists it is dry. The whole thing belongs to the past. When we let our minds run their own way, we tend to think in that fashion of the first great outflow of the Spirit of life, symbolized by the wind and the fire and by the water too.

If that be our mood, this text speaks to it. "This promise is unto you and unto your children and to all that are afar off." At least Peter thought that there was here implicitly the promise of an abiding experience as precious to the individual as to the Church. To him it was full of significance for all his hearers, shamed and baffled as they felt themselves to be, crying out, "What shall we do?" He was sure that this experience—"what ye both see and hear"—might affect them profoundly and was meant to cover a wide area.

"All flesh," "your sons and daughters," "young men and old," "slaves as well as free-men"—these were the prophetic words for which he claimed fulfillment at that moment. His eyes followed the successive generations—"your children"—and looked to the far horizons—"all who are afar off." He saw nothing limited or ethereal or ecclesiastical or unpractical in the promise as he gazed for a moment down the distant years and across the widening leagues. It was for their private need as they faced life and for succeeding decades.

The illustration I have used may help us to see how mistaken we are when we think of the Pentecostal experience as a thing of the past save in the sense that the fountain differs from its stream. It is quite true that the aqueducts are only melancholy noble reminders of the past with their broken arches and intermittent waterless channels. But Rome today is a city of fountains. That is one of its features. Just as in London we say that there is not a street from some part of which you cannot see a tree, so in Rome there is scarcely a street from which you cannot at some point see or hear the splashing of a fountain. Yes, the aqueducts are broken and useless, but the springs on the hills still flow, and the conduits, largely out of sight, bring the water unceasingly to the city.

A like truth is taught us by our text concerning the outflow of the Holy Spirit. Though the outward phenomena of Pentecost—the mighty rushing wind and tongues of fire—have passed away, the Church of Christ is still a city of fountains, the Spring in the eternal hills has never failed since it first burst forth. If Pentecost cannot be repeated, it can be perpetuated. The Pentecostal era is continuous as the stream from a newborn spring becomes continuous through the centuries.

It would indeed be untrue to deny that there have been repetitions of Pentecost in individuals. At intervals, sometimes long intervals, we find a special experience granted to special people which on a smaller scale resembles the communal experience at Jerusalem.

There is no more striking example than that of Blaise Pascal. This exceptional genuis, who died when only thirty-nine, invented the wheelbarrow and the omnibus, investigated the highest reaches of mathematics and advanced its bounds, wrote one of the most brilliant and finished satires in the world—*The Letters of a Provincial*—and one of the most fertilizing books on Christianity—his *Pensees*—this man had such an experience of which he has left a record. When twenty-five years of age he turned decisively to religion, but it was not till six years afterwards that he received, a baptism of the Holy Spirit. His record of it was found after his death. It was sewn into his doublet. Somewhat condensed, it runs as follows:

The Year of Grace, 1654,
Monday, November 23.
From about half-past ten at night to
about half-past twelve.
Fire! Fire! Fire!

36

God of Abraham, God of Isaac, God of Jacob,
    not of the philosophers and the savants.
        Certainty! Certainty! Joy! Peace!
            God of Jesus Christ.
        Joy! Joy! Joy! Tears of joy!

This is a very remarkable document and records
an experience answering to Pascal's deep sense
of need and his unqualified surrender of himself.
It was a repetition of Pentecostal blessing in
a single soul.

It is fair to say, too, that there have been
times in the history of the Church when the
winds of God have swept across some portion
of His people, bringing an immense renewal
of religious life, like a second springtime. In
such hours spiritual facts and spiritual forces
have compelled attention and Jesus Christ has
been throned afresh in many hearts and in the
community. For such a renewal of Pentecost
some of us look steadfastly, having more than
once felt the first breath of it in our nation,
only to see it die away again. We cannot tell
how or when it will come once more in full
force. "The wind bloweth where it listeth—so
is the Spirit."

But I am concerned at the moment to remind
you that in the absence of the dramatic manifestations of the power of the Spirit, we still live
in the Pentecostal era, and the promise is for
us and for our children. No one realizes rightly
what the Christian life offers and ensures until
he has come under the spell of this conviction.
A good many of Christ's people have not ac-
quired the habit of faith which relies on this
outward supply of energy and force for all needs
as well as for occasional emergencies. It is true
that all Christian people possess a vague confidence that behind our own personality there

lie the resources of God. But our temptation is to depend upon them only for the outstanding and sorest demands of life.

We regard the succor of the Holy Spirit very much as the Flemish folk in Balzac's tale regarded the hidden treasure provided by the countess who ruled them—as a last resource only to be drawn on under dire necessity. Her land was impoverished, her people dispirited, agriculture and commerce at the lowest ebb. To encourage them to labor and to venture, she assured them that she had provided a store of treasure which would support them through the worst disasters. But she asked a pledge that they would not open her letter of instructions or break into the coffer until every other expedient had been exhausted.

Her people took heart and toiled and planned as never before. Again and again, when harvests failed or ventures miscarried, the struggle seemed well-nigh hopeless, and they were on the point of reading the sealed document and resorting to the secret store. But always, supported by the assurance of it, they made one more effort. As the years went by, prosperity came, success outweighed failure, cities grew rich.

Long after the good countess had died, when all danger of bankruptcy and famine was past, the descendants of her subjects broke the seal and sought out the treasure. A rusted iron coffer, small in size and containing only a few hundred florins, was duly found. It was an infinitesimal store, which would have tided over only the smallest emergency. But the knowledge that there was something behind them had nerved them to continue when ready to succumb under struggle and anxiety.

In such a fashion many Christians believe

38

in the succor of the Holy Spirit. They never quite put it to the test. But the vague assurance that there are resources on which they may draw, if on the verge of despair, nerves them to continual striving after goodness and keeps them loyal to their ideals. Such buttressing of soul in the long struggle is not to be despised. But, if the treasure be not a slender store, if it be inexhaustible wealth, they might have gained a finer hopefulness and a stronger inspiration, which would have won a wider usefulness and a swifter victory.

God is merciful to our half-faith. We gain oftentimes subterranean succor, succor of which we are scarcely conscious, for we have never definitely or daringly asked for it. But God does not mean us to live in such a fashion. Verily He does not, my friends! "The promise is for us and for our children." We are meant to live in daily commerce with the base of spiritual supply. It is the divine intention that we should both attempt and achieve more than we do and the wherewithal has been provided in the divine Spirit. The Spring on the Eternal Hills still leaps and flows and overflows—it is the channels that are lacking, be they aqueducts above or conduits below the surface. That is the conviction I would imprint on your heart and on mine.

What does the availability of the Holy Spirit mean? It means inexhaustible resources to supply all kinds of moral and spiritual need. Are we in the path of God's will, living where He has placed us, dedicated to all He commands us? That is the preliminary question. When it is answered rightly, then we are justified in depending on the Holy Spirit to make us adequate to every demand, not only the sudden insurgent demands, but also the repeated and continuous demands to which we so often respond with weary or laggard feet.

We cannot exhaust our God. There is no anxiety in God. When we unite our exhaustion to His strength and our anxiety to His watchful wisdom, then in reliance on His resources things become possible to us which were impossible. Without breaking down, we are able to carry burdens which seemed well-nigh intolerable. What God wants us to do, He will enable us to do in the life within and the life without. This will not mean deliverance from all care, but it will mean deliverance from the most poisonous of anxieties—the fear that somehow God will let us fail in things essential to life. The Pentecostal Era (which is simply another name for the Christian era in which we are living) means sufficiency of strength for every God-appointed task, and in addition wisdom to detect and courage to refuse the tasks unappointed by Him.

Further, the availability of the Holy Spirit means reliable reinforcements. Who of us has not known some challenge of life which we could not refuse without dishonor, which yet demanded more than we had to give? We mustered our manhood to supply the demand, and there was not enough manhood to meet the challenge. We mobilized the support of our friends, but, do what they or we could, their support was insufficient.

Then one of three things happened. We accepted dishonor and put aside the challenge, perhaps pretending it was not there. Or we answered the challenge hopelessly and half-heartedly and were beaten. Or we put our trust in God, standing as we were on the verge of despair. Then something happened. Reinforcements flowed in. There was a change in the

40

converging circumstances or our own inward forces were steadied and strengthened. The accepted responsibility was rightly discharged, the arrogant temptation decisively overcome, the haunting shadows of failure dispelled. What made the difference? The power of the Holy Spirit! What He did for Peter He has done for us—transformed and reinforced us.

It was like walking a narrow path, up a steep hill, by the side of a precipice. The path led straight to a slippery plank, one foot broad, above an abyss. If we were to go forward, that was the only way. To go back was to be dishonored. We needed more than courage; we needed a steady foot, an eye that saw the plank and refused to see the abyss, a confidence that we could walk these yards of peril. All we can say is that we won this steadiness, this confidence, and we went forward without dishonor and without failure. Nothing can convince us that it was merely hidden resources in ourselves which reinforced us. No! it was the gift of God. We had depended on the unseen reinforcements of the Heavenly Energy, and they came. The promise was for us—yes, for us! That is the experience we are meant to know right to the end.

The Holy Spirit is available.

MAN'S NEED—
GOD'S GIFT

Malcolm McNeill Hare

If ye then, being evil, know how to give good gifts unto your children: how much more shall your heavenly Father give the Holy Spirit to them that ask him?

Luke 11:13

George Morrison, quoting this question addressed by the Master to His disciples, underlines the words 'bread . . . fish . . . an egg . . . the Holy Spirit,' and comments: "One must never forget that in talking of the Spirit our Lord deliberately passes by the luxuries, and chooses out things that are essential. For Him the Spirit was not, as it were, a luxury, the choice possession of a favored circle. It was not something that would enrich the life over and above the indispensable: it was the minimum of filial existence." The same truth could scarcely be put more bluntly than by the Apostle Paul in his letter to the Christians at Rome: "Now if any man have not the Spirit of Christ, he is none of his" (8:9).

The New Testament has much to say about the presence and purpose of the Holy Spirit in the world, but we need no more than a cursory glance at the context of this verse to discover how vitally important it is to know exactly what our relationship to the Holy Spirit is, for on that depends whether or not we have any right to the name 'Christian.'

Three thoughts are suggested by our text.

The Necessity of Having the Holy Spirit

That is first. As the context makes perfectly plain, we are not here dealing with luxuries. The Spirit constitutes "the minimum of filial existence." And that means that apart from Him there can be no saving relationship to *Christ*.

The question "What is a Christian?" is often asked and many sermons have been preached on the subject as well as many answers given to the inquiry. For an answer in a nutshell, what could be clearer or simpler than Paul's statement already referred to?

A Christian is a person in whose heart and life the Holy Spirit is. It is His ministry to make the Book live for every reader, to lead men into all truth, to take of the things of Christ and reveal them to us. His is the work of re-proving the world of sin, of righteousness and of judgment. Jesus speaks of "that which is born of the Spirit" (John 3:6); and in two other verses the Third Person of the Trinity is quite patently associated with the work of salvation. "But ye are washed, but ye are sanctified, but ye are justified in the name of the Lord Jesus, and by the Spirit of our God" (I Cor. 6:11). In the Letter to Titus we read: "Not by works of righteousness which we have done, but according to his mercy he saved us, by the washing of regeneration, and renewing of the Holy Ghost" (3:5).

Since His ministry is to glorify the Saviour, to point the sinner to the One who died on Calvary's Cross for the sins of the world, to reveal

43

the truth, to bring life from God and spread abroad in human hearts the very nature of God which is love, conviction and conversion are impossible apart from Him.

The necessity of having Him is emphasized not only by the fact that apart from Him there can be no saving relationship to Christ, but also by the fact that apart from Him there can be *no living resemblance to Christ.* There may be no solution to the problem of Predestination, but there cannot possibly be any argument about the purpose of it! "For whom he did foreknow," writes Paul, "he also did predestinate to be conformed to the image of his Son, that he might be the firstborn among many brethren" (Rom. 8:29).

In his exceedingly helpful book, *The Art of Sermon Illustration* (p. 75), the editor of this volume tells a remarkable story that unforgettably illustrates this point. In setting about painting his celebrated study of John Wesley, Frank O. Salisbury's first task was the gathering of as much material as possible about the subject. After closely examining the relics, pictures and a very lifelike bust of Wesley loaned by the Victoria and Albert Museum, London, in order to gain some idea of the appearance of the man and the impression he must have made on other people, the artist felt that there was still something missing. He needed a living model, someone much like Wesley and about the age at which he wanted to paint him—seventy-five.

He found that man in Charles Voysey, the architect, and when he asked for his cooperation, "he looked at me in astonishment," wrote the artist, "and said nothing would give him greater pleasure, for he belonged to the Wesley family." The family resemblance was there.

44

What is it that, above all else, God wills for His people? It is a life conformed to the image and likeness of Christ, not simply a life where Christ is present but a life where He is *seen* to be present, and that is impossible apart from the work of the Holy Spirit. "We all, with open face beholding as in a glass the glory of the Lord, are changed into the same image from glory to glory, even as by the Spirit of the Lord" (II Cor. 3:18). The One who brings the new life is the One who maintains it and so transforms it that in the life of His people Jesus is seen.

The Certainty of Receiving the Spirit

That is next. How compelling and reassuring is the argument of Jesus in this passage! The love for a child in the heart of a parent is the same the world over. It is as strong among the most primitive tribes as in the most civilized community, and in some cases maybe even stronger. "If a son shall ask bread of any of you that is a father, will he give him a stone? or if he ask a fish, will he for a fish give him a serpent? or if he shall ask an egg, will he offer him a scorpion?" asks Jesus knowing full well what the answer will be.

All true parents want nothing but the best for their children. They are prepared to sacrifice anything and even everything for the good of their family. "If ye then, being evil, know how to give good gifts unto your children: how much more shall your heavenly Father give the Holy Spirit to them that ask him?" It was out of love for the world, love that overwhelms by its length and breadth and depth and height, that God gave His only begotten Son, and it is for the same reason that He gives the Holy Spirit. "Like as a father . . . so the Lord," says the Psalmist. "If ye then, being evil, know how to give . . . how much more shall your heavenly Father give?" says the Lord.

This is a gift *God wants to give.* The parent desires to bestow upon his child nothing but the best which it is in his power to confer. So with God.

Alexander the Great was proud of the fact that his subjects could approach him at any time. On one occasion a beggar came to him with a request that some might have considered sheer impertinence. He wanted a farm for himself, a dowry for his daughter, and an education for his son. To the amazement of his court, Alexander granted the threefold wish, and when officials expressed their astonishment later, he replied: "Oh, I get weary of these people who come to me in their shoals asking for a gold piece. That saucy beggar treated me like a king. He asked big."

That is how God likes to give, and He has nothing bigger or better to bestow than the Holy Spirit, for when He gives the Spirit He is giving Himself. Since we cannot save ourselves, God has undertaken to do it for us, and He does it through the Spirit. It is by Him that we are brought into a saving relationship to Christ, and it is by Him that there is created in us a striking resemblance to Christ.

When you consider not only the fact of the Holy Spirit, but also His function, His fruit and His fulness, is it not obvious that the gift of the Spirit is the greatest that God can confer and the one that He wants to give?

Again, the gift of the Spirit is one that *God waits to give.* Some of God's gifts are bestowed indiscriminately whether or not men want them: not so the Holy Spirit. Children are not normally given food unless they are hungry and really

46

want it—and even sometimes, when they *do* need it, it is very difficult to get them to take it! Similarly, before the Spirit is given there must be a holy craving for Him.

Dr. Paul Rees tells of a rather unusual but nonetheless delightful incident that happened some years ago in the United States. After a few days of Convention a man approached one of the speakers to confess to him something of his own spiritual need. "My heart is so hungry," he said. "I need what you have been preaching about. God knows, I need the power of the Holy Spirit in my life."

After a few questions, the speaker told the man: "I believe I know where you could enter into blessing." "Where?" asked the inquirer eagerly. "Well, would you like to come with me?" "Yes, by all means." So they left the grounds of the Conference Center and began walking up a canyon.

As they walked and talked endlessly about the fullness of the Holy Spirit, every so often the man would ask: "Where is this place where I am to receive what I want?" "Oh, it isn't very far," his companion would say; "up here just a little bit." After going further, the man broke in again, "Wherever is this place?" and back would come the reply: "Oh, it is not very far now." At last the man exclaimed: "Listen! I cannot bear this any longer. I have got to have a meeting with God. I must be filled with the Holy Spirit." Then his friend said: "This is the place! Right here!" So together they knelt at the roadside, and for that person the place became Pentecost.

"Blessed are they which do hunger and thirst after righteousness: for they shall be filled," said Jesus (Matt. 5:6). When we are definite and desperate, God delights to give the Spirit, who changes creatures of God into children of God and begets in them the family likeness of heaven. Understandably, then, Dr. W. E. Sangster can write: "When you have the Spirit, you have everything worth possessing. The Holy Spirit is the greatest gift that God can give. When He gives the Holy Spirit, He gives all precious things with Him. When He gives the Spirit, He gives Himself." It is the gift He wants to give, but waits to give.

The Simplicity of Obtaining the Holy Spirit

That is last. After a night's fishing, when the nets were as empty as they were before they were cast into the Sea of Galilee, Simon Peter was returning to shore, a dejected fisherman. With the help of Jesus, however, who was standing on the beach and in obedience to the command of Him who called across the waters in the dim light of a grey dawn, he found that a shoal of fish was on the other side of the boat. Only a boat's-breadth away! That was all! And for the answer to defeat and dejection of many a human life created for higher things, the believing sinner and the sinning believer have neither far to look nor much to do.

The Holy Spirit is obtained initially by *the simple act of asking.* "Your heavenly Father," says Jesus, "gives the Holy Spirit to them that ask." That is all we have to do and it is the sheer simplicity of it that constitutes a stumbling-block for so many. They have not, declares James, because they "ask not" (4:2). Or if they ask and do not receive, it is because they do not ask in faith, believing that because they are asking what God wants to give they will surely receive. We can never earn this gift (it would cease to be a gift if we could!), neither can we ever deserve it. Convinced of our need of the Holy Spirit and yearning to have Him, we must come to God as we are and ask for the One whom the Father is anxious to bestow, and He will abide with us forever.

Professor Murdo Ewen Macdonald relates an incident which took place during the visit of D. L. Moody to Edinburgh. The great evangelist was having lunch with a minister of that city who, during the meal, indicated that he was very worried about a visit he had to pay that afternoon. Pressed as to the nature of it, he said that it concerned the delicate matter of approaching a rather formidable, wealthy lady in the congregation to ask her for a generous gift to help pay for work that urgently needed to be done in his church. "How much have you asked for?" inquired Moody. "Fifty to sixty pounds," replied the minister. After a moment's thought, his guest said to the minister: "Would you mind if I come with you?" Only too happy to have his company as moral support, the minister made answer: "Not at all. I should be very delighted, and so would the lady."

When they got near the house, Moody said to his friend, who had become noticeably nervous: "Do you mind if I do the talking?" Greatly relieved, the minister raised no objection. Once inside, and after formal introductions were over, Moody began: "Madam, we have come here today on the Lord's work. Our brother here is troubled about the paying for jobs that must be done in the church, and he has been asked to come to you for help. He tells me how you are blessed with this world's goods, and I want to ask you if, as a token of gratitude to God and His goodness to you, you will give me a check for two thousand pounds to lift the congregation out of its present difficulty." "Two thousand pounds!" she exclaimed. "Oh, Mr. Moody, Mr. Moody, I could not do that, but I will give you a check for one thousand pounds!" Moody was delighted; the minister almost fainted!

The Holy Spirit is the greatest gift that God can give, and when we ask for Him we are praying for that which God will not refuse. In clearest terms He says: "Ask, and it shall be given you" (Matt. 7:7). And in the words of our text: "If ye then, being evil, know how to give good gifts unto your children, how much more shall your heavenly Father give the Holy Spirit to them that ask him?"

If the Holy Spirit is obtained initially by the simple act of asking, He is enjoyed continually by *the sustained attitude of receiving*. As long as a glass full of water is held under a running tap the water will continue to overflow, and as long as the Christian remains in contact with the supply of the Spirit, out of him will flow those rivers of living water of which Jesus speaks in John 7:38, 39. Asking for the Spirit is not merely the initial act that brings Him into a life, it is the habitual attitude that keeps the soul open to His gracious ministry day by day.

It used to puzzle me why I should be urged to ask every day for that which I received at conversion. It seemed foolish, to say the least, if not also the betrayal of a lack of faith, to go on asking God to give me what I already had. But there is really no problem here at all.

On three occasions Paul speaks of the Spirit as the 'down payment' which the Christian receives, and in this age of hire-purchases and mortgages, most people can appreciate the figure.

50

The down payment means that there is more to follow, and that it will follow. Applying the analogy to the Holy Spirit, Paul links the life that the Christian now lives to that which he will live in the glory of the Kingdom of Heaven. According to Ephesians 1:14, the Holy Spirit is the guarantee of our inheritance until we acquire possession of it. Children of God, therefore, are to show in this present evil world what the future life will be like because they have already been granted a share in it by the presence of the Spirit in their lives.

When Christ is accepted, the Holy Spirit is imparted, and day by day it is the Christian's responsibility as well as his privilege to pray for the presence of the Spirit in ever-increasing measure—unceasingly and increasingly, in fact. Taking is just the other side of asking, and both together form not simply an initial spiritual transaction but the continuous spiritual experience which God wills for His people in the fullness of the blessing of the Holy Ghost.

"Bread . . . fish . . . an egg . . . the Holy Spirit." Necessities, not luxuries! The Holy Spirit is indispensable. Without Him no one can become a Christian, and without Him no one can become the Christian that he ought to be. Let me ask you: How is it with you today? Have you got Him? More important, has He got you? How little effort on our part could result in a tide of blessing and revival sweeping the world and, like the river in Ezekiel's vision, giving life to everything caught up in it!

"Raleigh, when will you stop asking?" said Queen Elizabeth I to Sir Walter, who had asked for yet another royal favor. Adroitly, Raleigh replied: "When Your Majesty stops giving."

The only time to stop asking God for the Holy Spirit is when He stops giving, and this

51

He will never do! Will you quietly appeal to Him again to fill you with His Spirit, and to do it now? If every Christian would do that every day, there would not be room enough for the blessing God would be pleased to bestow. Then the Church would begin once more to burn and blaze in witness to Christ, and the day would not be far distant when every knee would bow and every tongue confess that He is Lord of all.

PATTERNS AT PENTECOST
Michael C. Harper

As I began to speak, the Holy Ghost fell on them, as on us at the beginning. Then remembered I the word of the Lord, how that he said, John indeed baptized with water; but ye shall be baptized with the Holy Ghost.

Acts 11:15, 16

The early church had a vivid memory of Pentecost as well as of Easter. Ten years after that event, in the house of the centurion Cornelius, Peter remembered Pentecost when he saw and heard the same manifestations. "I remembered the Word of the Lord," he said. Some years later, when Paul was writing to Titus, he too remembered the pattern of Pentecost when referring to the Holy Spirit—"which he poured out upon us richly through Jesus Christ our Saviour" (Titus 3:6). The memory was sure, but it needed to be refreshed. "I remind you," wrote Paul to Timothy, "to rekindle the gift of God that is within you" (II Tim. 1:6).

The Church prospers or declines in its fortunes in proportion to its belief in and experience of the Holy Spirit. Writing in 1928, L. Elliott-Binns commented: "As one looks at the state of the Church today, its primary need is for power and that power can come from the Spirit alone."

There were patterns at Pentecost, although the details may vary from age to age.

In Worship

The coming of the Spirit provoked an immediate act of worship. This point can be easily overlooked. From the later Fathers onward the view has often been held that the gift of tongues was given for an evangelistic purpose—to bridge the language-barrier and present the Gospel to the heathen. A closer examination of the text will reveal that this was far from the main purpose of the gift. The audience gathered *after* the gift had been received, and in any case was mostly composed of Jews, so there was no language-barrier anyway. No, it was an act of worship! The language-barrier was between God and man, and this was the rapturous overflowing of love from hearts that had been touched by the divine presence, and found their own language inadequate for deep intercourse with their God.

There is a pattern here to balance liturgical worship. We could call it 'ejaculatory,' but it is part of the fibre of true worship. Notice how often Paul, for instance, suddenly breaks off his discourse in Romans and expresses spontaneous worship, as if he can only just about finish his sentence (1:25; 9:5; 11:33, 36; 16:27). The Spirit supplies the inspiration. The origin of much liturgical worship might well be traced to such spontaneous utterances.

There is a pattern here, too, of congregational worship. They *all* worshipped. There is no one-man band here, but an orchestra blending together in harmony. In some ways this was not new. Jewish synagogue worship followed this congregational pattern. When Christ, as a visitor, was asked to read and preach from the Scripture, it was the normal practice. How foreign the modern type of service, with a choir to sing and a minister to preach and pray, is from the exciting spontaneity of the early days! The ministry was to help in the building up of the Body of Christ—not to monopolize the worship!

There is also a pattern of God-centered worship. It really was 'divine service.' God was in the midst of His people, and they were "lost in wonder, love and praise." There was no sad preoccupation with man or introspective lamenting over sin, but free worship and love for God.

In Evangelism

The worship died down as the Church became aware of the inquisitive eyes of several thousand spectators. They were talking excitedly to one another. "What does this mean?" they asked. Others were sneering: "They have been on the bottle." Suddenly Peter and the other apostles got to their feet and turned to the crowd. Gone were the old fears of men. Gone was all self-consciousness. The first Christian sermon was preached spontaneously and without notes or preparation. God's program of evangelism had begun, and the first converts added to the Church. (N. B. There is no "counting of heads"— "*about* three thousand souls" is the modest estimate.) Peter was tactless enough to mention the Cross, and direct enough to blame them all for it! Here was no compromise.

There is much we can still learn from this pattern of most successful evangelism. There is still the need for the Holy Spirit to give courage, to inspire utterance, to banish fears, to convict men, to bring people to a place of decision, and to be relevant. Peter's sermon may not be an object lesson in homiletics, but it was very effective for all that.

55

In Ecumenism

Pentecost in some ways was the beginning of the ecumenical movement. The Church, however, was not then cursed with denominationalism. But there were equivalent barriers to be broken down. There seethed in the minds of Jews the most bitter resentment against the Romans. The Jews proudly regarded themselves as altogether superior to all other races and religions. "Dogs" was a common epithet to describe foreigners. There was also deep jealousy in the conflict between Jews and Samaritans. The differences were partly historical and partly doctrinal. The Jews preferred the hard dusty desert highway from Jerusalem to Galilee rather than pass through Samaria. Imagine, too, the feelings of the early Christians for those who had cruelly and falsely accused, brutally whipped and ruthlessly murdered their best Friend—One whom they had worshipped. They, too, were human.

But now suddenly all is different. These murderers are brothers. They worship with them, eat with them, take Communion with them, pray with them—yes, and share their possessions with them.

Pentecost is a pattern for ecumenism. The Holy Spirit came as fire and purged the Christians of pride and self-glorying. Their past traditions counted as nothing, if they got in the way of fellowship with those who were their former enemies. The walls came tumbling down. First, Jesus' murderers, then hated heretical Samaritans, then radically corrupt Gentiles. Each time it is the Holy Spirit, as Acts unfolds its story, who is the Agent. They are baptized in His love and power. There is only one way to join steels together—to melt *both*!

Pope John once said: "For the renewal of the Church, there must be a new Pentecost." For the early Christians Pentecost supremely meant *freedom*. "Where the Spirit of the Lord is, there is freedom," wrote Paul (II Cor. 3:17). The pattern we have seen is not a rigid system of theology like others which have tended to enslave their adherents and separate them from everyone else. It was freedom to worship God— from the heart as well as from the head. Liturgy is fine, so far as it goes. But every liturgy needs to be supplemented and the worshipper who uses it transformed by the free Spirit of God.

Pentecost spells freedom to evangelize— freedom from self-conscious fear of men, what they think, say or do. It means freedom to proclaim God's Word without compromise. The Spirit gives this confidence. Pentecost means freedom to be the Body of Christ—not just in theory, but in practice; to share utterly; to count nothing "one's own"; to create a caring society in striking contrast to a selfish one. The Holy Spirit did it then, and He will do it again in our day.

Pentecost was love "poured out"! Not sentimentalism, but divine love. Not feelings and mystical experiences, but a practical outflowing love for God and all men.

THE GIFT OF FIRE
John Henry Jowett

*He shall baptize you with the Holy Ghost
and with fire.*

Matthew 3:11

Such is the divine promise. Let me read the
story of its fulfillment. "And when the day of
Pentecost was fully come, they were all
with one accord in one place, and suddenly there
came a sound from heaven, as of a rushing
mighty wind, and it filled all the house where
they were sitting. And there appeared unto them
cloven tongues, like as of fire, and it sat upon
each of them."

Here, then, are men and women who are
about to receive the promised gift of the Spirit
of God. They had been waiting, as their Master
directed; waiting in prayer, and in prayer in-
calculably strengthened by community of desire, waiting in trembling watchfulness and expectation. Then the much-hoped-for day arrived
and their spirits received the infinite reinforce-
ment of the gift of the Holy Spirit. What happens
to the human spirit is suggested to us under
the familiar symbols of wind and fire. "Like
unto a rushing mighty wind"; "like unto fire."

Do not let us be enslaved by any hampering
details in the figures. Let us seek their broad
significance. And what is the characteristic of
a rushing mighty wind? It dispels the fog. It
freshens the atmosphere. It gives life and

nimbleness to the air. It is the minister of vitality. The breath of God's Spirit is like that: it clears the human spirit, and freshens it, and vitalizes it; it acts upon the soul like the air of a spiritual spring. And as for the symbol of the fire—fire is the antagonist of all that is frozen. It is the antagonist of the torpid, the tepid; it is the minister of fervor, and buoyancy, and expansion. The wind changes the atmosphere, the fire changes the temperature; and the Holy Spirit of God changes the atmosphere and temperature of the soul. When you have changed the atmosphere and temperature of a soul you have accomplished a mighty transformation.

It is about this change in the moral and spiritual temperature that I want to meditate— the gift of fire which we receive in the baptism of the Holy Ghost. If the spirit of man and the Spirit of God come into blessed communion and the fire of God is given, how will it reveal and express itself? For if there be a gift of fire in the soul we shall most surely know it.

First of all, I think I should look for the holy fire on the common hearthstone of human life.

If the fire of God does not warm up the affections I fail to recognize what its heat can be worth. The first thing to warm up is the heart. The intimate friend of the Holy Spirit is known by the ardor of his affections. He loves with a pure heart fervently. He is baptized with fire. Now I need not seek to prove the existence of cold hearts among us. I am afraid we must accept them without question. Whether there are hearts like fire-grates without a spark of fire I cannot say. Personally, I never met with anyone in whose soul the fire of love had gone quite out. I think that if we sought very diligently among the grey dusty ashes of any

burnt-out life we should find a little love some-
where. Yes, I am sure we should. But there
are surely souls so cold and so destitute of love
that the poor fire never leaps up in dancing,
cheering, welcome flames. Their temperature
is zero.

There are other souls with a little fire of
love burning, but it is very sad, very sodden,
very sullen, very dull. There is more smoke
than fire. There is more surliness than love.
Their fire is not inviting and attractive. There
is a little spitting and spluttering and crackling,
but there is no fine, honest, ruddy glow. Their
temperature is about ten above freezing. They
are not frozen, but they are not comforting.

There are other lives where the fire of affection is burning more brightly and certainly
with more attractive glow, but where it seems
as if the quality of the fuel must be poor because
the fire gives out comparatively little heat. The
heart sends out a cheery beam across the family
circle, but it does not reach beyond. There is
no cordial warmth for the wider circles of fellowship. The fire burns in the home, but it does
not affect the office. It emcompasses the child,
but it has no cheer for the stranger.

What awfully cold lives there are in this great
city, just waiting for the cheer of "the flame
of sacred love"! There are souls whose fires
have died down at the touch of death. There
are others whose glow has been dulled by heavy
sorrow. There are others whose love has been
slaked by the pitiless rains of pelting defeat.
There are others again whose hearts are cold
in the midst of material wealth. They have richly
furnished dwellings, but their hearts are like
ice. They are unloved and unlovely, frostbitten
in the realms of luxury. Wealth can buy atten-

tion: it can never purchase love. My God, what cold souls there are in this great city!

And, therefore, what a clamant and urgent need for love-fires at which to kindle these souls that are heavy and burdened and cold. And when the Holy Spirit is given to a man, and he is baptized with fire, it must surely, first of all, be the fire of cordial human affection. And such is the teaching of experience. When John Wesley came into the fullness of the divine blessing in a little service at Aldersgate Street, London, he said that he "felt his heart strangely warmed." He was receiving the gift of the holy fire.

You find and feel the glow of that love-fire throughout the New Testament Scriptures. They who have the most of God's Spirit have the most of the fire. The truth of the matter is this, we cannot be much with the Spirit of Christ and not take fire from His presence. In these high realms, communing is partaking, and we kindle the same affection as fills the heart of the Lord. "We love because he first loved us" (I John 4:19). His fire lights our fire and we burn in kindred passion. So do I proclaim that when the fire of God falls upon our spirits the sacred gift kindles and inflames the soul's affections. When we are baptized with the Holy Ghost and with fire we receive the glowing power of Christian love.

Where else shall we look for that holy fire in human life? I think I should look for the presence of the fire of the Holy Ghost in fervent enthusiasm for the cause of Christ's kingdom.

And that indeed is what I find. The New Testament instructs me in this, and it teaches me that when a man is baptized with the Holy Spirit and with fire, his own spirit becomes fervent. He is declared to be "fervent in spirit," and the original word means 'to bubble up,' 'to boil' as in a boiling kettle. It is the emergence of the mighty power of steam. And so the significance is this: the fire of God generates steam; it creates driving power; it produces forceful and invincible enthusiasm.

You will find abundant examples of this Spirit miracle in the Acts of the Apostles. Perhaps the book might be more truly named "The Acts of the Holy Spirit," for all the glorious activity is generated by His holy fire. Let your eyes glance over the apostolic record. Mark how the fire of God endows man with the power of magnificent initiative. Take the apostle Peter. Once his strength was the strength of impulse—a spurt and then a collapse, a spasm and then a retreat, proud beginnings bereft of patience and perseverance. But see him when the Spirit of God has gotten hold upon him, and what a gift he has received of initial and sustained enthusiasm. "And Peter, filled with the Holy Spirit!" You should see him then, and note the strength of his drive and the ardor of his enterprise.

The first apostles drove through tremendous obstacles. Indeed, they never had the comfort of an open and unimpeded road. Every road was thick with adversaries. What then? Through them or over them! "But, Sire," said a timid, startled officer to Napoleon on receiving apparently impossible commands; "But, Sire, there are the Alps!" "Then there must be no Alps!" replied his audacious chief.

"There must be no Alps!" That was the very spirit of the first apostles. Mighty antagonisms reared themselves in their way—ecclesiastical prejudices, the prejudices of culture, social hostilities, political expediencies, and all the subtle and violent contrivances of the world, the flesh and the devil. "But, Sire, there are the Alps!" "There must be no Alps!" Through them! Over them! What that coward Peter got through when the fire of God glowed in his soul! When a man has the holy fire of God within him he has a boiling fervency of spirit and he can rise through anything.

That same holy fire is the same terrific power today, the same driving enthusiasm, the same patient, dogged, invincible perseverance. If a man declares that he has received the fire of God's Holy Spirit, I will look eagerly for the impetus of his sacred enthusiasm. If he be a preacher, I will look for labor in passion and the unsnarable energy and patience which he will assuredly put into his work. If he be a teacher, I will examine the generated steam, and note how much he can do, how far he can travel and how long he can hold out in the service of his Lord. If he be a man who has set himself to some piece of social reconstruction, I will watch with what ardor and ingenuity and inevitableness he is moving towards his goal. Whatever it be, the holy fire of God will reveal its presence in the soul of man in an ardent enthusiasm which cannot be quenched. It is the promise of our God, and shall He not do it? "He maketh his ministers a flaming fire" (Heb. 1:7), and that fire can never be blown out in the darkest and most tempestuous night.

And, lastly, I shall look for the sign of the presence of the Holy Spirit in the fire of sacred resentment.

If a man is baptized with the Holy Ghost and with fire, I shall expect to see the presence of that fire in the capacity of hot and sensitive indignation. I need not say that there is a mighty difference between hot temper and hot indignation. Hot temper is a firing of loose powder up on a shovel. It is just a flare and an annoyance and a danger. But hot indignation is powder concentrated in the muzzle of a gun and intelligently directed to the overthrow of some stronghold of iniquity.

What is this capacity of indignation? It is the opposite to frozen antipathy, to tepid curiosity, to sinful 'don't-care,' to all immortal coldness and calculated indifference. There are many people who can be irritated, but they are never indignant. They can be offended, but they are never nobly angry. The souls who are possessed with the fire of God are the very opposite to all these. I said at the very beginning of the meditation that the breath of God is like the quickening atmosphere of the spring: but it is equally true to say that it can be like the destructive blast of the African sirocco. "The grass withereth and the flower fadeth because the Spirit of the Lord bloweth upon it" (Isa. 40:7).

The hot breath of God is like a blast that scorches things in their very roots. And if we share in the breath of God's Spirit we too shall be endowed with the ministry of the destructive blast, the power of a consuming indignation. Any form of public iniquity will make our fire blaze with purifying wrath. Corruption in civic or national government, inhumanity in the treatment of the unfortunate and the criminal, the oppression of the poor, the brutal disregard of the rights of the weak and the defenseless —any one of these will draw out our souls in the hot and aggressive indignation which is the imparted fire of the Holy Ghost. If anyone claims to have been baptized with the Holy Ghost and with fire, and he is indifferent in the presence of licensed iniquity, and apathetic and lukewarm when gigantic wrongs glare and stare upon him, that man's spiritual baptism is a pathetic fiction, and his boasted fire is only a painted flame.

But if a man suffer a personal injury, if some wrong is done to him, what kind of fire shall I expect to see in his life if he is filled the Holy Ghost? Yes, if someone has done an injury to another and the other has been baptized with the Holy Ghost, what kind of fire will he reveal? "Then said Jesus, Father, forgive them, for they know not what they do." What kind of fire is that? It is the same holy fire which flowed from the soul of the martyr Stephen as he was being stoned to death: "Lord, lay not this sin to their charge." It is a marvelous fire, a most arresting fire; and we simply cannot withstand it. It is the very fire of grace; it is live coal from the altar of God.

So this is the sort of fire I look for when a man claims to be filled with the Holy Spirit —the glowing fire of humble affection, the glowing fire of noble enthusiasm, the glowing fire of indignation, and the marvelous fire of self-forgetting grace. "He shall baptize you with the Holy Ghost and with fire."

INTERIOR REINFORCEMENT
Kenneth J. Macdougall

Strengthened with might by his Spirit.
                              Ephesians 3:16

But have not all Christians been "strengthened with might by his Spirit in the inner man"? Apparently not, for Paul is in fact praying for his fellow-Christians. He is not praying now for the unconverted, but for those who have already received the Gospel and put their faith in Christ.

Moreover, Paul is praying for a definite gift for his brethren. He is not asking for some vague, indefinite blessing to which in course of time they might one day aspire. His careful use of the aorist tense in the text implies a definite action, in which the longed-for blessing is given and received.

But let us look a little closer at Paul's request.

First, he is asking that his Christian brethren may be strengthened with *might* or *power.* Power is, of course, one of the great characteristics of the truly Christian life. For many, alas, Christianity is 'just words,' but the great apostle reminds us that "the kingdom of God is not in word, but in *power*" (I Cor. 4:20). John Wesley used to ask his Methodists if they had a sense of the power of God in their lives. But not all who could testify to the forgiveness of sins could speak of the power of God within, and the same is true of many Christians today. That is why we need to be strengthened with power.

Secondly, Paul prays for power where we need it most—"*in the inner man.*" What a man is within the inner recesses of his life is the true measure of the man himself. If, as Christians, we are weak within our inner being, we shall not only be poor samples of our Lord, but vulnerable to every temptation we meet. The inner citadel must be strong.

But *how* are we to be strengthened within our inner being? Not by trying harder! Not by screwing up our will! Not even by the rigors of religious discipline! Only by the power of the Holy Spirit can it be effected. So Paul writes: "Strengthened with might *by his Spirit* in the inner man." That is the petition the apostle urgently presents.

What is it that prompts Paul to ask for this gift of the Spirit? Why does it fall as the first of his petitions here? Because this is a gift highly necessary in itself and the precondition of everything that follows.

Take, for example, his next request: "That Christ may dwell in your hearts by faith." This cannot be fully experienced until we are first strengthened with power. Let me again remind you that Paul was writing to Christians. Every Christian knows something of the indwelling Christ. Our trouble is that we know only 'something' and not really what Paul is praying for, which is, that Christ may dwell, not as an intermittent guest (present when our faith admits Him and absent when our self-love excludes Him), but dwell as the permanent Host inhabiting every room. This is what our Lord referred to in His discourse on the Holy Spirit when He said: "If any man love me, he will keep my words, and my Father will love him, and we will come to him and make our *home* with him" (John 14:23). Permanent and complete!

The same is true of Paul's next request: "That you may have power to comprehend the *love* of Christ." The word 'comprehend' means more than 'to perceive.' It means 'to grasp' (NEB) or 'to lay hold upon,' really to make our own. But, as the apostle states, this is not something that we can do in our own strength or even acquire through discipline and self-denial. We must have *power* to comprehend. Sin has weakened us so much that even as Christians we may be like someone recovering from a protracted illness, who is thereby precluded from the greater part of life because of weakness. Everything depends upon being strengthened with power.

Now there are some Christians who, oddly enough, look with suspicion upon any thought of a further gift of the Spirit over and above that normally received at conversion. They affirm (rightly) that we receive the Holy Spirit at the moment of our regeneration and deduce (wrongly, as I believe) that there is nothing more to receive. They are in error. Not only would that deduction make nonsense of Paul's prayer, but it is contrary to the teaching of the New Testament as a whole. Jesus Himself was endued with power (Acts 10:38). His truly human nature needed to be empowered. His disciples were commanded to wait for power (Luke 24:49). And Paul was "filled with the Holy Spirit" under the ministry of Ananias (Acts 9:17).

When we have been "strengthened with might by his Spirit in the inner man," these other great experiences which Paul includes in this sublime prayer come within our grasp. I do not say that we have "arrived," or that we need no longer watch and pray; but I do say that God has now set before us the path to the peak of Christian perfection.

Christ now really dwells within us, but no longer as a transient Guest. He is an abiding Presence, the Lord of every motion of our hearts. Think of the saintly Oswald Chambers, struggling for years with a sub-Christian faith and almost ready at one point to call the whole thing a fraud. But after what he later described as his baptism in the Holy Ghost, he wrote: "Glory be to God, the last aching abyss of the human heart is filled to overflowing with the love of God. After He comes in, all you see is 'Jesus only, Jesus ever.' "—Oswald Chambers, *Life and Work* (London: Marshall, Morgan & Scott, p. 50)

The same is true of the love of Christ that passeth knowledge. Now, at last, we grasp it! The Holy Spirit is the Spirit of the love of God, which no man can *win* or achieve no matter how hard he tries. If mere discipline could have won the love of God, John Wesley would have certainly succeeded, but the first part of his life was clouded with failure. Fast and pray as he would, the love of God eluded him. After that gift of the Holy Spirit fell upon him in Aldersgate Street, however, "old things passed away, behold they became new." Now he is no more lugging and carrying about a riddled bucket of piety, no sooner filled than emptied again. The love of God is poured into his heart by the Holy Spirit given unto him, and upon this river he is borne into all the world. This was the secret shared by the first Methodists. How right was he who said that the secret of Christian living is not *overwork*, but *overflow*!

We come, then, to this crucial question:

How? *How* can we receive this gift of the Holy Spirit? *How* can we be "strengthened with might by his Spirit in the inner man"?

Before coming directly to the answer, there is one thing we must get clear. *We must desire to be!* This is no light thing to ask of God. Let us be sure what we are about. A. W. Tozer writes: "To the interested inquirer I put these questions: 'Are you sure you want to be possessed by a Spirit who, while He is pure and gentle and wise and loving, will insist upon being the Lord of your life? Are you sure you want your personality to be taken over by One who will require obedience to the written Word? Who will not tolerate any of the self-sins in your life—self-love, self-indulgence? Who will not permit you to strut or boast or show off? Who will take away the direction of your life from you and will reserve the sovereign right to test you and discipline you? Who will strip away from you many loved objects which secretly harm your soul?' "—*Keys to the Deeper Life* (p. 28)

These questions must be settled before we proceed. The Holy Ghost is the Spirit of fire. He will not be trifled with.

That surrender having been made, however, we must *ask* for the Holy Spirit. Sometimes we must be willing to go on asking, for only so can we prove the sincerity of our request. But, long or short, it is certain that we must ask. So often we have not because we simply do not trouble to ask. The promise is to them that ask. "If ye, then, being evil, know how to give good gifts unto your children: how much more shall your heavenly Father give the Holy Spirit to them that ask?" (Luke 11:13).

Then, finally, we must *believe.* "This only would I learn of you," writes Paul, "received

70

ye the Spirit by the works of the law, or by the hearing of faith?" (Gal. 3:2). Faith does not ask for the impossible: faith believes the promise. If we ask for bread, God will not offer us a stone; and if we ask a fish, He will not offer a serpent. Faith *believes* the promise, and believing *is* receiving. "If ye, being evil, know how . . . how much more will your heavenly Father *give* the Holy Spirit?" Ask, then, and receive the promise. "It is God's nature to give Himself to every yearning soul," says Meister Eckhart. "Know then that God is bound to act, to pour Himself out into thee as soon as ever He shall find thee ready." "Ask, and it shall be given you; seek, and ye shall find" (Luke 11:9).

THE DAY OF PENTECOST
F. B. Meyer

This is that.   Acts 2:16

The day of Pentecost has been described as in a sense the birthday—*dies natalis*—of the Holy Spirit. His mission was to constitute the Church as the Body of Christ, to rule and guide it, to add to it those who were being saved and to reveal to them things which eye has not seen, nor ear heard, nor the heart of man conceived, but which are made known to those who are led by the Spirit.

The events of that momentous day are headline news in the Book of Acts. Suddenly over an upper room of Jerusalem, where one hundred and twenty disciples had been gathered for ten days, there was a startling burst of sound. It seemed as if a terrific whirlwind had swept down upon the city. Yet not a leaf was quivering, not a tree swaying. The sound had been like that of a violent blast of wind, but clearly this was no natural tempest. It was a supernatural invasion, a penetration of history by the powers of the world unseen. On the disciples in the Upper Room the Holy Spirit descended, filling the house, filling themselves, filling the world.

So excited and exuberant were the followers of Jesus that disaffected onlookers dubbed them drunken. Peter had no difficulty in rebutting

that absurd charge, pointing out that the pubs
were not yet open! And, in beginning his discourse, he made the dramatic announcement:
"This is that" (Acts 2:16).

What Was This?

For ten days, as we have noted, the one
hundred and twenty loyal souls had awaited
the gift of spiritual power which their Lord had
promised. Each day as it passed witnessed the
same absorbed expectancy. "Not many days,"
the Lord had said, and so any day might be
the one on which the gift would be conferred.
For the world's sake, and for their own, they
had continued to claim the fulfillment of the
promise and to rid themselves of every conceiv-
able obstacle to its reception.

It would appear that on this festival day
when in the temple the priests presented the
first loaves of the new harvest to God, the disciples had risen from their knees and were sitting in an expectant attitude. Then suddenly
they saw tongue-like flames distributing themselves, one resting on the head of each, and
they were all anointed and filled with the Holy
Spirit. The same experience befell them as had
befallen their great Leader when He was baptized. That had been His Pentecost, as this became their baptism. Each looked at his companion, admiring on his head the halo of fire,
but never suspecting that there was one on his
own!

From the beginning the Holy Spirit had
brooded over the chaos of the elements and
of human society; but now for the first time,
as we have seen, He created the nucleus of
the Body of Christ and laid the foundation of
the one holy, mystical Church, according to

Christ's word: "I will build my church and the gates of hell shall not prevail against it" (Matt. 16:18). Such was *this*.

That, on the other hand, was the prediction of the prophet Joel, who foretold that the hour would come when slaves and slave-girls would break forth into prophecy; and that, amid the convulsion of nature and the falls of empires, vast numbers would call on the name of the Lord and crowd through the gates of salvation. In the scene before him Peter perceived the actual fulfillment of that ancient prophecy; the fulfillment, too, of the Saviour's promise that His disciples would receive power, the power of the Holy Spirit, coming upon them.

This Is Not That

The professing Church of today is far removed from its Pentecostal prototype. *That* was united: *this* is divided into a number of warring sects. *That* was full of triumphant joy; *this* has to have professional choirs to sing for it. *That* set little store by material wealth: *this* pays court to it. *That* was marked by simplicity of method: *this* substitutes paid agents to perform the work of evangelization and soul-winning. *That* was a commonwealth of mutual happiness: *this* permits class distinctions and observes them. No greater contrast between *that* and *this* could be adduced than the brief sentences which describe the Church's infancy, when the Lord added to it daily those who were being saved, and the endeavor of large numbers of Christian communities which attract congregations by ornate ritual or popular oratory or adventitious attractions. There are, to be sure, significant exceptions, where churches are still crowded and the people hear a live Gospel. Generally speaking, however, with the dismal statistics of dwindling church attendance and membership before us, we are sorrowfully compelled to confess that *this is not that.*

This Might Be That

The apostle did not say that Joel's prophecy was fulfilled. He clearly realized that the scene before him was only the first installment towards its fulfillment. The gift of the Holy Spirit has never been withdrawn, and indeed miracles are happening today in the hearts of men and women no less wonderful than those which took place in the past. The river of God flows on in glorious fullness, but the professing Church has removed from its banks and is creating a new settlement on the edge of a desert. It is forsaking the fountain of living waters for cisterns that can hold none.

Yet an instant alteration might be effected if only the leaders of the churches, ministerial, lay, and indeed the membership as a whole, would turn once more to those stores of blessings which await us in "the residue of the Spirit."

Here are two instances from modern church history which encourage the faith that God's arm is not shortened that it cannot save, nor His ear heavy that it cannot hear.

The first is the familiar case of John Wesley. He met Peter Bohler, a Moravian, at a religious gathering in Aldersgate Street, London, and afterwards accompanied him to Herrnhut in Germany, where, on the invitation of Count Zinzendorf, the consecrated and missionary-hearted Moravian Church had found its home. It was there that he entered the experience of Pentecost, and on his return to London invited the Aldersgate group to meet him one afternoon at the Moravian Church in Fetter Lane. Present at that memorable service, in addition to him-

self, were his brother Charles, George Whitefield and others whose names were destined
to shine as stars. After they had continued for
some hours in fellowship and prayer, they became conscious of the mystic presence of the
Holy Spirit and fell on their faces in reverent
worship. After a while they got up and sang
the *Te Deum*. On the next morning Whitefield
took the early coach to Bristol, and the great
revival, whose celestial flame saved Britain
from the fires of revolution, broke out.

The second instance relates to D. L. Moody.
As I was sitting with him one Sunday morning
under the veranda of his home in Northfield,
Massachusetts, he gave me the following account of an experience he had had. Shortly after
his conversion he took the big market-hall in
Chicago and gathered a vast crowd of hearers
for his Sunday evening service, but with comparatively small results. A group of Christian
women used to occupy the front seats, and as
he came down from the platform would say
to him something like this: "Very good, Mr.
Moody, very good! But there is something better
and we are praying for you." He wondered what
they meant. Wasn't the hall crowded? Were
there not signs of God's blessing in renovated
lives?

One summer afternoon, however, as he was
passing along Fifth Avenue, New York, he felt
that he must get alone with God. So he went
to the house of a friend and asked for the use
of a room where he would not be disturbed.
Putting aside offers of hospitality and refresh-
ment, he locked the door against interruptions.
In that sacred hour he yielded his whole being
afresh to Christ and received the baptism of
power. On the following Sunday evening the
Spirit of God so moved on the congregation

that afterwards the women who had been praying for him said with tears and smiles: "Ah,
Mr. Moody, you have got it now!" That was
the beginning of a mighty ministry for which
his biographer was later to claim that in point
of results it was unmatched in the history of
the Christian Church.

This Shall Be That

Why should not every one of us arrange to
spend one day at least alone with God in quiet
self-examination? Why should not each of us
put to himself the pointedly personal inquiry:
"Am I experientially possessed of the Pentecostal enduement? Am I willing to pay the
price of it? Am I prepared, if needs be, to
surrender reputation, position, even the favor
of our immediate clientele, in order to receive
it?"

A story is told of a man who fell down a
well, but managed to grasp the end of a sus-
pended rope. He held on in the dark until his
strength gave out, and then found that he had
only six inches to drop!

How often we dread letting go! But it is only
when we have let go and let God that we find
peace and power.

Yes, we must let go and — we must take
in!

I trust I shall not be charged with egotism
if I relate the following narrative recounted by
Wilbur Chapman: "Two or three years ago Mr.
Moody invited me to breakfast at his home in
Northfield. I got to the house before the breakfast hour and met F. B. Meyer beneath a great
tree in front of the house. I said to him: 'What
is the matter with me? So many times I seem
half empty and so many times utterly powerless
—what is the matter?'

"He put his hand on my shoulder, and said: 'Have you ever tried to breathe out three times without breathing in once?' I wondered if he was referring to some new breathing exercise, so I said: 'I do not think I have.' 'Well,' he said, 'try it.' So I breathed out once, and then I had to breathe in again. Then he said: 'You must always breathe in before you can breathe out, and your breathing out must always be in proportion to your breathing in.' Then he said: 'Good morning!' and I went on into Mr. Moody's house. But I had had my lesson, and I knew that I had been trying to breathe out more than I had breathed in."

Is not that the trouble with so many of us? We have not recognized that that is the principle of spiritual as of natural respiration. We must inhale to exhale. We can only breathe out as we breathe in.

THE MEANING OF PENTECOST

Thomas A. Smail

You shall receive power when the Holy Spirit has come upon you. Acts 1:8

They were all filled with the Holy Spirit. Acts 2:4

A promise is made and ten days later it is fulfilled. But what on earth does it all mean? Calvary we know—its pardon and its purging; Easter we know—its joy and its hope; to the fact of the Gospel we can answer with our personal testimony. But we are all at sea with Pentecost. This has never happened to us. The Book of Acts opens with a weird and rather frightening experience that lies right outside contemporary Christian expectation. And so often on Whit Sunday the perplexed congregation asks the equally perplexed preacher: "What does it mean to be filled with the Spirit of God?"

To clear the ground of possible misunderstandings, let us look, first, at three things it does not mean.

To begin with, it does not mean that these people had an overwhelming but temporary emotional experience that can largely be accounted for in psychological terms. Obviously, they did have that. Whatever hit them that morning hit them so hard that at first it left them dazed and apparently drunken. They were stirred to the depths of their being in a way that was both cleansing and energizing; a way that so purged them and empowered them that they could only talk of it in terms of fire that means purging and of wind that means power. But, although it started with this overwhelming moment of ecstasy, it was far more than that. These men were not stirred and inspired for a moment only, they were changed for a lifetime.

What it means to be filled with the Spirit is not described or contained in the two verses that tell of their first great experience. It is something that takes the whole of the Acts of the Apostles to tell, the whole life of Peter and John and the rest to unfold. This was not just a moment of surpassing emotion: it was to stop being one kind of Christian and to become another instead.

But also to be filled with the Spirit does not mean speaking with tongues. Those who speak most in our day of the filling of the Spirit are sometimes thought to be unduly concerned with what is its normal accompaniment in the New Testament. Partly by their own fault and partly by the misunderstanding of others who fasten on to what is unfamiliar to them, they are taken to be running a movement for the promotion of universal tongues-speaking among modern Christians.

Of course, the apostles at Pentecost did speak with tongues. The second half of our text makes that quite clear: "They were all filled with the Holy Spirit and began to speak with other tongues as the Spirit gave them utterance." One of the first effects of the Spirit upon them was to give them a new language, new words welling up from the depths of their hearts in praise of God. Those who contest the possibility or actuality of that—then or now—are quarreling with God's Word. But speaking with tongues was the least of what happened to them that day. This is only one minor effect of the coming of the Spirit.

Many have been filled with the Spirit and for various reasons have never spoken in tongues, although they have been the poorer for the lack of it; and it is a strange Christian who has no interest in any gift, however strange and seemingly uncongenial, that God through His Spirit offers to His people. But when we are thinking about the fullness of the Spirit, it is foolish to get bogged down in discussions for or against tongues. There are far mightier and more vital things at stake here for the Church of Christ.

But there is a third thing that being filled with the Spirit does not mean: that they became Christians for the first time that day. Before Pentecost these men followed Jesus; they claimed and accepted the pledged pardon of Calvary; they companied with the Risen One; they confessed Him Lord and God. "He who believes and is baptized will be saved" (Mark 16:16). A saving relationship with God rests on a trusting faith in what Christ has accomplished for us on Calvary, and the specific Pentecostal element does not at that point enter into the picture at all.

If any man ask how he may become a Christian, how he can be saved, our answer will not be "Be filled with the Spirit," but always and first "Believe on the Lord Jesus Christ." What happened at Pentecost is a second to that first. Calvary precedes Pentecost in fact and in faith alike, and until a man has been to the Cross he has no part in the Spirit. The promise of power is a consequence of, and by no means a substitute for, the promise of pardon. Christians are *equipped* at Pentecost: they are *made* only at the Cross.

But "what God has joined together, let not man put asunder." Those who have been at Calvary are also called to Pentecost. You can be a genuine silver teapot, and yet never have tea infused in you or poured from you. You can be a house that is purchased by somebody so that there is no doubt who holds the deeds of ownership, and yet that house can stay empty and never be occupied and possessed. But why make the teapot if it is not to be used? Why buy the house if it is not to be possessed? So a Christian can be born of the Spirit without being filled with the Spirit. He can believe in what Christ has done *for* him without going on to receive what Christ can do *in* him. He can open his heart to Christ's promise of pardon and yet close his ears to Christ's promise of power. When that happens, God's purpose in that man has been prevented from reaching its fulfillment; God's intention for that man has been frustrated; that man has taken the "so much" that comes from Calvary, but has not yet taken the "so much more" that comes from Pentecost.

When Christ's people thus stop short of Pentecost, you have that ambiguous thing which is one of the banes of all the churches in our day—the powerless believer. He knows quite well what Christ has done for him; he knows, too, that he has not got what it takes to get on and do it—he is powerless. He loves the Lord, he is a believer, but he is not living for the Lord—he is powerless. He lives by forgiveness of sin, he is a believer, but he knows that the very things that have been forgiven still have their power over him unbroken—he is powerless. He accepts in the most orthodox way possible all the signs and wonders of the Gospel, he is a believer, but "greater works than these shall [you] do" (John 14:12) he neither believes nor expects to see happen—he is powerless. His Christ is at the right hand of God and to Him all power is given, but his church is losing out to the world on every hand. The call to prayer and the call to witness to which such promises are attached have become to him a matter of reproach and shame, for he is capable of neither. Of the powerless believer we can each complete the description for ourselves, for what we are describing is just our own state in all its frustration and failure.

Lack of power—though we believe in Christ's power! Lack of life—though we believe in Christ's life! And all because, on the clear word of Jesus, we have stopped short of Pentecost. "You shall receive power when the Holy Spirit has come upon you" (Acts 1:8). This is the specific gift of the Holy Spirit in His fullness; not emotional moments, not merely or mainly supernatural gifts, not saving grace, but this other thing that we so lack—energizing power to be God's people to do God's work, to be what Christ has made us, to do what He has sent us to do.

At Jesus' baptism in the Jordan the Holy Spirit came in His fullness—power that was not needed in the same measure when He was the carpenter's Son at Nazareth, but power that is now to be needed in full measure when He starts His work as the anointed Son of God. Power with God, so that whatever He asks of the Father is given to Him. Power with men and with the world, so that there is immediate recognition of His authority in the crowds, with

83

the evil spirits, even with the winds and the waves of Galilee. Power with Himself to conquer the tempter, to integrate and employ all the energies of His being in His great work, to offer Himself in the fullness of His sacrifice. He comes and He works and He dies in the power of the Spirit He has received.

But in the Gospels His disciples just stand around and support and spectate. They cannot pray as He prayed; they cannot heal as He healed; the evil spirits are not subject to them; there is no power of love in their lives to change and transform the publicans and sinners. In the garden and in the high priest's courtyard it is their weakness and not His kind of strength that prevails. Powerless believers indeed were they!

But "you shall receive power"! Nothing that was His would He keep to Himself. Just as the pardon of His Cross was not for Himself but for them, so the power of His Spirit was not for Himself, but for them. And on the day of Pentecost, in a definite act of impartation as decisive as any sudden conversion, that power which up to then had been only His became theirs as well. "You shall receive"—and there and then they did receive—"power." "They were filled with the Holy Spirit" (Acts 2:4). To put it crudely but clearly, the thing that made Him 'tick' gets into them also and makes them tick that way too. These men are given the whole supernatural resources that Jesus had before them—for their dealings with God, for their dealings with men, for their dealings with themselves.

In his new power Peter preaches and three thousand are converted. In their new power Peter and John bid the lame man at the temple gate rise and he rises. In their new power these men are joined together in a love that has all things in common and that irresistibly reminds those who see them of Jesus. In every city they enter there is either a riot or a revival. Both when they accept it and when they fight against it, men are conscious of something they cannot ignore in these apostolic messengers that come to them—the power of God.

With the Spirit come His gifts—tongues to pray in, prophecies, wisdom, knowledge to discern their work and their mission, healings, and deliverances as they are needed to defeat the powers of darkness—the Spirit against the spirits. In these men the fruit of the Spirit forms and grows and ripens—love and joy and peace and self-control, and so on. And the key to it all and the entrance to it all is Pentecost. These now are not just men who believe certain things about Jesus: they are men who receive things from Jesus. The Spirit that is in Him is now in them.

On the day of Pentecost Peter offers this power—not to finished saints but to newborn believers; not to one dispensationally favored generation, but to all Christians in every place and in every age. "You shall receive the gift of the Holy Spirit. For the promise is to you, and to your children, and to all that are far off, *every one* whom the Lord our God calls to him" (Acts 2:38, 39). If you have come to Christ, then the Spirit is come to you in this fullness, in this power. You are to have, as surely as the pardon of the Cross, this prevailing boldness in prayer, this effective boldness in doing God's work among men, these gifts to exercise in His service, this fruit to grow in your own life to His glory. "Your heavenly Father is willing to give the Holy Spirit to them that ask him" (Luke 11:13). He is Christ's Spirit and

He belongs to all who are Christ's. If we struggle on somehow without Him, it is not because He is not offered but because He has not been received, because the faith that we exercised in accepting what was offered at the Cross, we have not yet exercised again to accept what is offered in the Spirit.

You don't need to go on glossing over your failure in prayer, in Christian work and witness, in the fight against self and sin, as if there were something wrong with you or something wrong with the Gospel. As in a definite act of seeking and taking, you made the pardon of Christ your own, so in another definite act of seeking and taking you may make the Spirit of Christ you own. He has promised, and that promise has been kept all through the years and will be kept again "to every one whom the Lord God calls to him." "You"—and it means *you*!—"shall receive power when the Holy Spirit has come upon you." Claim that, take that, and indeed you will know what it means to be filled with the Holy Spirit.

FIRE IN THE BONES
Gordon Strachan

If I say, "I will not mention him, or speak any more in his name," there is in my heart as it were a burning fire shut up in my bones, and I am weary with holding it in, and I cannot.
Jeremiah 20:9

It was no fun speaking the Word of God in the days when Jerusalem was conquered by Nebuchadnezzar and her inhabitants were taken captive to Babylon. The judgment that would eventually overcome the Holy City had been prophesied a hundred years before by Isaiah and now the final stages of the tragic drama were being worked out. Jeremiah had been given the same message as Isaiah—that God would give personal and political safety in return for obedience, but that He would bring personal and political disaster if His people continued to disobey Him.

This was an unpopular message because by this time the judgment of God seemed much more obvious than His mercy, and the people didn't like it. Jeremiah told all the people that the coming destruction of the city at the hand of the king of Babylon was God's judgment, because they were proud and refused to obey His commandments. For saying this, he was beaten by the Chief Officer of the temple and put in the stocks. It was after this humiliating experience that he cried out his anguished prayer to God: "O Lord, Thou hast deceived me, and I was deceived. Cursed be the day on which I was born. Why did I come forth from the womb to see toil and sorrow, and spend my days in shame?" (Jer. 20:7, 14, 18).

He honestly thought God had let him down. He was utterly miserable. He hadn't wanted to be a prophet anyway. He had been quite content to be a humble young minister at Anathoth. He had told God he was far too young and inexperienced to get involved in the political turmoil of the day. Why hadn't God let him alone to get on with routine church duties in his hometown? If He had really called him to be a prophet to the nations, why had He gotten him into all this trouble? His family thought he was odd, his friends denounced him, and both priest and politician branded him a traitor, a fifth columnist for the enemy.

Finding himself in such a position of public shame and scorn, and even fearing for the safety of his life, the reluctant prophet would gladly have withdrawn from the scene—gladly gone back home, away from it all. The depth of his anguished cry to God makes us wonder why he stayed on in the thick of the battle to see the miserable calamity through. He surprised himself perhaps when in a brief moment of assurance he sang: "Sing to the Lord; praise the Lord! For he has delivered the life of the needy from the hand of evil-doers" (Jer. 20:13). But more than that so very brief song of gladness in the midst of all his turmoil, there had come to him the terrifying realization that even if he did want to get away from the whole wretched business, God Himself would not let him.

Part at least of Jeremiah's agony was that he was bound far more than he knew or desired to the powerful purpose of God. The same word which was hot on his lips in the divine correction of others also burnt passionately within him. Even he, the anointed prophet, could not escape the judgment if he, like his fellow countrymen, disobeyed the Master. He tried to quench the Spirit within him, tried to break free, but the fire of God could not be put out. It burned deeply in him. He had fire in the bones and it was all God's doing. "If I say, 'I will not mention him, or speak any more in his name,' there is in my heart as it were a burning fire shut up in my bones, and I am weary with holding it in, and I cannot."

During the season of Lent, when we prepare for Good Friday and Easter Day, we are tempted to reflect on the passion of Jesus in a passive mood. We become awed, even emotionally numb, as we try to appreciate and understand the mystery of this great and wonderful sacrifice. The heart of our faith and salvation is a marvelous mystery which we shall never fully understand, but we shall come nearer to understanding it and to a living faith if we try to see Jesus in the context of His times and as in the line of the great prophets of His national past.

Like Jeremiah He had fire in His bones— the fire of His Holy Spirit conception and Holy Spirit anointing. Like Jeremiah He often felt like giving up, found the going too hard, prayed in anguish of Spirit that God His Father would make it easier for Him. Like Jeremiah's, His family did not know what to make of Him, His friends turned away from Him, and both priest and politician plotted His downfall. Like Jeremiah He lived in violent times when another occupying army marched the streets of the Holy City and where within a lifetime the inhabitants of Zion would once again be put to the sword and scattered to the four winds. Like Jeremiah, Jesus displayed a strange combination of resignation and resistance towards the violence and destruction of the men around Him. Like Jeremiah, Jesus lashed out with His tongue against the hypocrisy and deceit, the intrigue and spiritual impotence, of those who stood for what was officially good—the establishment line.

Jesus Christ will come alive to you this Lent, this Good Friday, this Easter, if you see Him as a human character. It is just as amazing that He was a man as that He was God. If you don't believe He wanted to escape, like Jeremiah, from the shame and scorn of public disgrace, hear Him pray in utter anguish of Spirit: "Father, if it be thy will, take this cup away from me" (Luke 22:42). And see the sweat falling off Him like drops of blood.

If you thought Jesus was understood by His family, remember the incident when His mother and brothers stood outside and asked to speak to Him. When He was told, He said: "Who is my mother? Who are my brothers?" (Mark 3:33) and, pointing to His friends, He said: "Here are my mother and my brothers" (v. 34).

If you thought Jesus had staunch friends, then hear Him say to Judas: "Judas, would you betray the Son of Man with a kiss?" (Luke 22:48). And "they all forsook him and fled" (Mark 14:50).

You know how one and all conspired against Him, but had you thought what a violent, tumultuous week our Holy Week was, and how so soon after they had turned away from the salvation of Christ, a violent end came once again to the Holy City? God in Jesus Christ had presented His people once more with the same challenge as He had given them with Jeremiah—personal and political salvation through faithful obedience, personal and political destruction through disobedience. The tragedy that overtook the people, the priests and the politicians who turned away from the word of Jeremiah, is written large on the pages of ancient history. But the spiritual and national disaster that followed Jerusalem's rejection of Jesus Christ was ten times greater. Fortunately, this was not the end of the story.

The Gospel of Jesus Christ comes to us as a violent remedy to a violent situation. In a day when we are all threatened by nuclear war and destruction at the mass level, we cringe at accepting God as fire to answer fire. Both Jeremiah and Jesus knew that at heart mankind is desperate, violent and bent on self-destruction. The truth of their insight is written large on the pages of history before and since. It is shatteringly true today. And yet many Christians seem to be unaware or uncaring concerning the urgency of the crisis. They are like the religious people of Jeremiah's time who said complacently: "Our God will protect us whatever happens" and who mocked the prophet when he shouted "Violence and destruction!" They are like the religious people of Jesus' time who kept to the other side of the road when crime was rampant and who preferred to see the Church running smoothly rather than be upset by the eccentric compassion of this Galilean who lashed them with His tongue.

Television, radio and press keep us in touch with the world's activities as never before. We cannot plead ignorance of the nasty side of life that cries to us for redemption. Yet our main concerns are indistinguishable from the unbeliever's—a higher standard of living and domestic security. Most of us, when confronted with the world's need, say that the problem is too big for us. "What can I do about it anyway?" we ask, and we use this as an excuse to justify our non-involvement. This is why in so many cases the Church is regarded as irrelevant to the major issues of the contemporary world. And what greater issue needs to be examined in the light of the Cross of Christ than the violence of our times?

In one Glasgow hospital in one year there were 1031 cases of stabbing admitted. In the decade 1956-66 there was a 67 percent increase in crime. The total jumped to 104,000 cases. During the years 1961-66 the crime figures increased by 152 percent. The weekend bus curfew in Glasgow following the teenage murder of a bus conductor was just one more case.

What is the point of Christians interesting themselves in the times of Jeremiah or of meditating on the passion of Christ if there is no link between the past and the present, between faith and action?

Since coming to the East End of Glasgow four years ago, I have become involved in the crime and violence that stalk the streets of our asphalt jungle. When I first witnessed an act of violence on one of the streets of my parish, I watched horrified and frightened on the other side of the road. What does a young inexperienced minister do on the scene of a crime? When I sat in on the trial of one of my parishioners accused of police assault, the sheriff asked me what sentence I would recommend. Was the answer leniency or severity? When fellow-Christians tell me I am wasting my time when I talk to the local gang at the corner, am I to think they are right or wrong? When a man comes to me very worried because he has lost his friend's jemmy, do I sympathize with him and help him to find it? When I have five teenagers in the vestry on a Sunday night for a chat and they all have police records, how do I commend to them the saving mercy of Jesus Christ?

I am convinced by my experience as a Christian minister that God comes to us today in a situation of crisis as Fire answering fire. I am convinced that, though our reluctance to do God's will be as great as Jeremiah's and our sense of personal inadequacy be even greater, God's fire only burns in us when we are in places where we are at the point of the world's need.

The passionate cry of Jeremiah tells us that the compassion of God was greater in him than his own desire to escape. The passion of Jesus Christ tells us that the Fire of God burns most strongly at the point of the world's dereliction. Whether you know it or not, whether you like it or not, we live in times like the times of Jeremiah and Jesus Christ—times as desperate and as violent. The only answer to the violence of men is the violence of the Gospel. God's remedy is as drastic as it always was, either obediently to share in His passion and compassion for the world or to suffer His judgment. The only power strong enough to tame violent men is the violent application of the Gospel. It is this radical step that we are unwilling to take—so that in spite of unparalleled advances in social welfare, society is powerless to prevent the rapid rise in crime. Only those who have the Fire of God in their bones are adequately equipped for this work.

Have you this Fire, this passion, this compassion? Is the Spirit of Christ in your guts? Are you on fire to meet this need in spite of your feelings of personal reluctance? Can you say with that valiant prophetic soul: "If I say, 'I will not mention him, or speak any more in his name,' there is in my heart as it were a burning fire shut up in my bones, and I am weary with holding it in, and I cannot"? The saving Fire of God took Jeremiah to the stocks and to prison. It took Jesus to the Cross. For the Christian also, who would save the masses, there is no escape when the same fire burns.

It is the same fire we must have today to save God's world from its own violence and destruction. Jeremiah lived through the disasters of his time until the realization came to him that God would bring back the defeated exiles into their own land and allow them to rebuild the Holy City and the temple. Jesus Christ lived through the violence of His own death to rise again and show that the destruction of man was not as powerful as the redeeming power of God. This power is still available to us today. It is most urgently needed. It is the redeeming power of God in Jesus Christ. It is the Fire of God, the Fire of the Holy Spirit. He does not promise to make it easy for us. If it was hard for Him, it will be hard for us. But He promises to be with us and in us and to conquer in the end if we will involve ourselves in His battle.

I have found that, in spite of my own hesitation and in spite of many failures, the power of God is still at work if His compassionate and refining Evangel is faithfully proclaimed. I have seen situations of imminent violence change to moderation because the Word of God has been spoken. I have seen lives of violence gradually change to order because of caring confrontation with the compassionate Christian. I have also watched something of a silent rebuke

come to those Christians who believed the violent to be outside the power of redemption. I
have also watched the embarrassment, uneasi-
ness and guilt of those who have heard the
truth, but do not wish to follow it. I have also
seen with sadness some who have attempted
to change, but have fallen back.

In all these cases I have seen enough to
convince me that the power of man to destroy
is not as great as the power of God to recreate.
I am glad I am in a situation where the way
of the Cross is meaningful and where the application of the Fire of God can cauterize the
wounds of human violence. I believe that our
prayer to God should be that He would kindle
such a fire in our bones that we may burn passionately for Him in His violent world. If He
was prepared to die for it, we should be prepared to live for it. In the last analysis, the
only fight it is right to fight is the good fight;
and, as Jesus rose from the dead, so He will
also bring us to victory.

On the violent streets of our violent city I
find the fire of God still burning—burning to
bring violent men to the peace of God, burning
to send men of God to proclaim the full salvation
of Jesus Christ to a world in urgent need. We
have the experience of Jeremiah. We have the
salvation of Jesus Christ. We have the power
of the Spirit. We have the fellowship of Christians. Now is the time to put faith into action.
We have all the armory we need. If the fire
of God is in your bones, then the battle is already
on. You are in the firing line. Your ammunition
is the Gospel. The command is "Fire!"

THE SEAL OF THE SPIRIT

Arthur Skevington Wood

> *In whom you also, who have heard the word of truth, the gospel of your salvation, and have believed in him, were sealed with the promised Holy Spirit.*

Ephesians 1:32

Paul was writing to a commercial city, so he used commercial language. His meaning would be easily grasped in Ephesus. It was a widespread custom in those days to affix a seal to a letter, a decree, an edict, a title of possession, or a piece of merchandise to give it validity, to prove its ownership and to ensure its safety. Nowadays the personal signature has superseded the old-fashioned seal. Just as today no check, no will, no agreement, no treaty is valid without the signature, so then no transaction was effectual without the seal.

In this passage Paul does what he has often done before. He lifts a word from the everyday world and baptizes it into a Christian meaning. If the associations of this term were commercial, the apostle's application of it was not. He made a tiny parable of it and employed it to typify the believer's experience of the Holy Spirit. We shall do well to dwell on it and to ask ourselves whether it finds a correspondence in our own heart and life. For it is only in the power of the Pentecostal equipment that we shall be prepared for work and witness in the Church. All that God requires of us will seem altogether beyond our capacities unless we realize that we have been sealed with the Spirit.

Before we proceed to examine the significance of the seal itself, it is to be noted that the Holy Ghost is given in Christ. Paul has referred to that memorable day when the Ephesian Christians trusted in Christ. And he goes on, still speaking of our Lord, "In whom you also . . . were sealed with the promised Holy Spirit." As Bishop Moule observed, the blessing of Pentecost is here regarded as "an additional aspect of the privilege of union with Christ." God has nothing for us outside Christ—not even the Holy Spirit. So closely is this experience linked with conversion that Paul alludes to it in the same breath: "In whom you also, who have heard the word of truth, the gospel of your salvation, and have believed in him, were sealed with the promised Holy Spirit." That might well be rendered "on believing you were sealed." The believing and the sealing are simultaneous. "While in order of salvation, sealing follows believing," explains Oswald Sanders, "in order of time, they come together in one combined transaction."

What, we may now inquire, is the meaning of Scripture here when it speaks about being sealed with the promised Holy Spirit? Taking up the analogy from the realm of commerce, let us interpret it in spiritual terms. It has much to teach us about our inheritance as Christians who have received the gift of the Spirit.

In the First Place, the Seal Is an Attestation of Reality

It gives validity to the document to which

it is attached. It is a guarantee of genuineness. Whenever the Pope makes a statement or issues a decree, he affixes his own special seal—the mark of the fisherman's ring—in order that all may know that it really comes from him. On the seal there are a number of curiously arranged dots: the particular way in which they are set is proof against forgery. The papal seal is known by the Latin word *bulla*—that which is embossed. Hence we hear of papal bulls: their authenticity is attested by a seal.

The same connotation is discovered in the Bible. When Jezebel was plotting the murder of Naboth the Jezreelite, and wanted to send letters in the royal name to the city elders, we are told that she not only wrote in Ahab's style, but "sealed them with his seal" as well, to supply the final touch of verisimilitude. The seal is an attestation of reality.

That is exactly the function of the Holy Spirit in the believer's life. It is He who gives validity to Christian experience. He sets to His seal that God is true. He glorifies our Saviour Christ. He ratifies the Word of truth, the Gospel of our salvation. He supplies the blessed assurance in which we are always to rejoice. "The Spirit himself bears witness with our spirit, that we are the children of God" (Rom. 8:16). As John Wesley declared in his famous sermon on this text from Romans: "One might say the testimony of the Spirit is an inward impression on the soul, whereby the Spirit of God directly witnesses to my spirit that I am a child of God; that Jesus Christ hath loved me and given Himself for me; and that all my sins are blotted out and I, even I, am reconciled to God." "An inward impression on the soul." What is that but a seal?

The seal of the Spirit assures us of a present

salvation and of eternal bliss, even though the conflict may still be raging around us. When a peace treaty is signed all the apparatus of war may still be in evidence. The troops may remain at their stations until demobilized. All the outward and visible signs may indicate that the struggle is continuing. But to every regiment there has been made a statement under an official seal, declaring that the conflict is to close and peace to begin from an agreed date and hour. It is a guarantee of the reality of an armistice, even in the midst of warlike surroundings.

So it is with the Holy Spirit of promise. He guarantees the reality of our reconciliation with God, even in this present evil world. In this case, the fight will not cease until death, but the seal of the Spirit assures us that we are on the victory side. How that should enhearten us when the going is hard and the outlook seems grim!

Again, the Seal Is an Indication of Ownership

It was often used to stamp personal possessions. Just as the shepherd placed his own secret sign on every sheep, so the Roman noble was in the habit of setting his private seal on his goods and chattels, so that it might be known whose they were. It was a mark of property.

This practice extended from material belongings to persons. Prisoners were branded: slaves were tattooed: soldiers were stamped: even women and children were mutilated in this manner. It was, moreover, a common feature in primitive religion that the worshipper should be marked with the likeness of his pagan god. The Greek historian Herodotus described a temple in Egypt at which a fugitive, taking sanctuary, might receive some physical incision, which indicated that he belonged to the god and was therefore not to be touched. It was because of these widespread practices in heathenism that the Israelites were forbidden to imitate them lest they should be contaminated. "You shall not make any cuttings in your flesh on account of the dead, or tattoo any marks upon you: I am the Lord" (Lev. 19:28).

It would seem, however, that it was known for men to carry the marks, not indeed of false gods, but of the true. There was a certain man of the sons of the prophets who disguised himself with ashes on his face so as to cover, it was supposed, the sign on his forehead which showed that he belonged to Jehovah. The prophet Isaiah anticipated the time when "this one will say, I am the Lord's . . . and another will write on his hand, The Lord's"; and in the visions of Ezekiel, the man with the inkhorn is commanded to go through Jerusalem and set a mark on the foreheads of the men who sigh and groan over all the abominations that are committed there.

Whatever may have been the Old Testament customs—and it is not suggested that they were universal—there can be no question that, for Christians, the Holy Spirit takes the place of those marks of ownership and allegiance. The seal of the Spirit testifies that we belong to God. When He is stamped upon us, then everybody knows whose we are and whom we serve. There can be no hiding the fact. Sometimes timorous believers prefer to remain incognito. They are afraid to stand up for Jesus. They keep their religion to themselves. In the eyes of the world they try to appear as others. They do not display the seal of the Spirit, for then all their friends would know that they are followers of the despised and rejected One. That is not Bible Christianity. That is not real Christianity. We should not be ashamed to own our Lord. On the contrary, we ought to be proud of our colors and eager that all should know that we are His and He is ours. The seal of the Spirit assures us that He claims us for His own. Let us not be guilty of disowning Him who has borne such shame in identifying Himself with us.

Furthermore, the Seal Is a Designation of Office

In New Testament times the appointment of a new official could not be announced to the general public inside a few hours as it can today. There were no newspapers, no railways or airlines to carry them, no telegraph service, no radio or television to reach every home. How were the inhabitants of some outlying Roman colony to recognize their new governor when he arrived? They had never seen his face or his portrait. Would it not be a simple thing for an impostor to seize the reins of government? Yes—but for one safeguard! The representative of the emperor was recognized by the seal he bore. That seal accredited him to his office. When in Rome he had little need of it; but when he went to a distant place, it declared the dignity of his post.

God has called us to bear our witness to Christ in a hostile world. We are chosen to be soldiers in an alien land. Our generation has largely forgotten God, and turned away from Christ and His Church. We are the King's messengers—ambassadors for Christ. But the world refuses to recognize us. We are treated as the scum of the earth and the dregs of humanity. We may even be tempted to wonder whether,

101

after all, we have any right to be invading the privacy of those who are so obviously apathetic and even resistant, as we seek to press upon them the claims of our Lord and Saviour. At such times we feel our need of a seal to attest our true standing before God. The one guarantee of our position as sons and spokesmen of God is the Holy Spirit. "For all who are led by the Spirit of God are the sons of God" (Rom. 8:14). Christ Himself carried this authorization: "For on him hath God the Father set his seal" (John 6:27). We may enjoy the same privilege as the Saviour-Son.

That is why the Christian can endure ignominy and insult without resentment. However harshly men may treat him, he knows that his commission is from God. The seal of the Spirit designates him to his high office. Men may still deride him and turn a deaf ear to his message. But he has no doubts about his status before God. So he can contemplate even his most formidable despisers with a kind of holy detachment, knowing that, if they are rich, so is he; if they are influential, so is he; if they are men of breeding, so is he in Christ.

But there is a further confirmation of the Spirit's seal. It is found in our fruitfulness, despite all the enmity and opposition of the world. Our own Christian experience is immeasurably enriched as, one by one, others are brought to Christ through us. Nothing in all the world can compare with the thrill of soul-winning. It is of this evangelistic corroboration that Paul speaks when writing to the Corinthians: "If to others I am not an apostle, at least I am to you: for you are the seal of my apostleship in the Lord" (I Cor. 9:2). He can look at his converts and declare with thankfulness of heart: "You are my seal." Can we do the same? Or must we confess that we have not yet ventured so far in personal evangelism?

Finally, the Seal Is a Guarantee of Protection

When a Roman official was dispatching his goods on a long sea journey, he marked them all with his seal so that they might be properly looked after. There, amongst the cargo, were the boxes bearing a special seal: they would be treated with particular care. Should the ship spring a leak or be endangered in any way, those boxes would be the first goods to be saved. Should the ship go down, those cases will be the first to be salvaged. The seal marked them out for special protection, and every human effort would be made to ensure their safe delivery.

So it is with the seal of the Spirit. Christians are exposed to the same risks, the same trials, the same temptations as others. But they are the objects of guardian care. The whole power of God is on their side, ensuring that they will be delivered from anxiety or distress, from moral harm or spiritual declension. God's mark is a guarantee of protection. In Ezekiel's vision, which we have already considered, the man with the inkhorn who sets a sign on the foreheads of the elect, is closely followed by a gang of merciless assassins who are permitted to wreck the divine vengeance on the iniquitous city. "Slay old men outright, men and maidens, little children and women: but touch no one upon whom is the mark" (Ezek. 9:6). In the book of Revelation, the one hundred and forty-four thousand are sealed by having the Father's name written on their foreheads. And as many as are sealed are saved. The seal is a guarantee of protection. Believers indwelt by the Holy Spirit are secured by sovereign love.

In Paul's day (as in ours also) the heathen put their trust in amulets and charms to ward off the evil influence of demons. Magical prescriptions would be inscribed on them, and always the seal of the demon would be included in the formula, so that men might be delivered from its malignant power. The faith that was placed in such worthless objects was considerable and pathetic. In *The Bible in Spain* George Borrow recorded a conversation he once had with a gypsy called Antonio. "I have no fear," the gypsy claimed. "The dark night is the same to me as the fair day, and the wild carrascal as the market-place; I have got the *bar lachi* in my bosom, the precious stone to which sticks the needle." "You mean the lodestone, I suppose," commented Borrow. "Do you believe that a lifeless stone can preserve you from the dangers which threaten your life?" "Brother," he replied solemnly, "I am fifty years old, and you see me standing before you in life and strength. How could that be unless the *bar lachi* had power?" Then he went on to catalog all the narrow escapes he had had, and concluded: "Were I in the midst of the gulf of Bombardo without a plank to float upon, I should feel no fear; for if I carried the precious stone it would bring me safe to shore. The *bar lachi* has power, brother."

Antonio had tremendous faith in his lodestone, but it was misplaced. Only one *bar lachi*, only one seal, can afford complete protection, not *from* adversity but *in* adversity, not *from* death but *in* death, and that is the indwelling Spirit of promise. It is with this ample protection that we face the challenge of our times, and go out to fight a host of foes.

There, then, are the privileges of those who are sealed by the Spirit. In the fourth chapter of Ephesians Paul urges his readers not to grieve the Holy Spirit of God, in whom they are sealed for the day of redemption. That fixes the intermediate position of this sealing. For "redemption" here means "our final liberation" (NEB), the complete emancipation of the saints at the end of the age—when the Lord has returned—and their elevation to glory. Until we sit in the heavenly places with Christ Jesus, we are given the seal of the Spirit as our surety that one day where the Master is there will also His servants be.

What an encouragement that is in the midst of all our toil and strife! The seal of the Spirit, it has been said, takes us to Mount Nebo where we may view the Promised Land in all its splendor. It brings us the grapes of Eschol, the specimen fruits of glory yet to be. It shows us the end from the beginning. It takes us, like Abraham, beneath the stars of heaven, and tells us: "This is your inheritance." Must we not, then, inquire within, and ask ourselves whether in fact we are rejoicing in this Pentecostal blessing, which has been bestowed on us in Christ? Just as Christmas means nothing to us unless Christ is born in our hearts and Easter means nothing to us unless He is risen in us, so Whitsuntide means nothing to us unless the Spirit has taken up His abode in us. If we have not yet appropriated what God means us to enjoy, let us seek it now.

THE PROMISED POWER
John L. Wynne

Ye shall receive power after that the Holy Ghost is come upon you.

Acts 1:8

When our Lord spoke these words to His disciples, He was undoubtedly looking forward to Pentecost. He knew that on that day a change would take place within them which would enable them to go out into the great world and do His work gloriously and effectively.

As you and I look back to Pentecost we can see that that was in fact what did happen on that day. Weak people were suddenly made strong. Ineffective people were suddenly made effective. Lukewarm people were suddenly set on fire. The Holy Ghost came upon them, as their Lord had promised, and they became filled with a new power which was evident to everyone.

For a very long time, the Christian Church looked back to Pentecost as being purely an experience of the past. In sermons, in Bible studies and in talks, the phenomena of the day of Pentecost were spoken of as things which happened once and for all.

Today, however, the Church is beginning to think otherwise. Those who are in touch with the spiritual movements at work in the world at the present time are aware that there is a Pentecostal outpouring taking place within the older denominations, the like of which has not been known since New Testament days. We are hearing from many parts of the world of ministers and lay-folk of every denomination coming into a deeper level of spiritual experience which is for them nothing short of a personal Pentecost.

Surely no one would dream of saying that the time is not ripe for such an outpouring! We are only too well aware of the powerlessness of the Church at large. We hear of great denominations reporting declining numbers year after year. We hear of dwindling congregations. We hear of people drifting, some towards humanism, and of many who are wandering around looking for an anchor for the soul.

How significant it is that in this particular situation God should be working in such a way to bring renewal to His largely powerless Church! What He is doing is in effect to restore the Holy Spirit to His rightful place and function. He wills that a powerless Church shall become powerful. Thus Jesus says to us as He said to His first disciples: "Ye shall receive power after that the Holy Ghost is come upon you."

First, Pentecost Means Power for Living

Look at what the restoration of Pentecost would mean to the Church of Jesus Christ! Pre-eminently, it would mean a new power for personal Christian living.

The disciples did not have a very high standard of Christian living before Pentecost. They quarrelled, they harbored petty jealousies, they talked of who should have the best seats in heaven, they cursed, they became easily embittered, they sent little children away, they slept in the crisis hour in Gethsemane; and, in the darkest hour of all, as their Lord faced the Cross, they forsook Him and fled.

Pentecost changed everything. From that day on, life was lived at a new level. They were still men of like passions to other people, but empowered as they were by the Holy Spirit, they were able to live victoriously, triumphantly. So much so, that others could not fail to mark the difference in them.

As we read the Acts of the Apostles and take a look at these people, do we see a rather wide gap between the Church then and the Church today? If we do, then surely we need to pray that this Pentecostal outpouring to which we have referred should flow through the entire Christian community, so that the Church of Jesus Christ in our time shall become as dynamic a force as she was in her earliest days.

How many of us have been "going it alone," as if there were no Holy Spirit available! We have acknowledged Christ, most of us. We have come to His Table, many of us. We have called ourselves Christians, a good number of us. Yet we have struggled on, largely in our own strength, and how often we have been only too conscious of our impotence! We felt as if we were alone.

Here is a picture of London in the late summer of 1940. France had fallen. Britain was facing the enemy alone. There was talk of an invasion of the south coast of England, which nearly came. There was talk of heavy air-raids on London, which certainly did come. A number of Londoners were feeling the weight of these events. One of them was traveling on the Underground, when suddenly at a station there walked into the train a uniformed Canadian airman.

The Londoner looked at him. He thought: "Canada is with us: The Commonwealth is with us! Men of goodwill all over the world are with us! London is not alone." And he walked out of the train at the station and passed into the street with a new lilt in his step.

Pentecost means something like this for us. It means that we need not face the battle alone. We need never feel isolated. We may ask Him to come in and take full possession of us, as He took full possession of those first Christians, and we may then venture forth with a new lilt in our step.

Do we wonder how we may reach this level of Pentecost? There is no level of spiritual experience which may not be ours, if we will but do what Jesus told us when He said: "Ask, and it shall be given you; seek, and ye shall find; knock, and it shall be opened unto you" (Luke 11:9).

Again, Pentecost Means Power for Witnessing

The restoration of Pentecost would mean new power for witnessing. No one can read the Acts of the Apostles without observing what a witnessing community they were. They were not timid. They were not shy. They were not ashamed of Christ. They were not afraid to talk to anyone about Him. Even when some tried to suppress them, they replied: "We cannot but speak the things which we have seen and heard" (Acts 4:20). Also, when warned of what would happen to them if they persisted in speaking about Jesus they answered: "We ought to obey God rather than men" (Acts 5:29).

What a revolution would take place if you and I were to begin to witness as they did! Nobody would talk anymore about "dying churches" if the Church today were to have to the witnessing level of the infant Church of the New Testament. We should shake the world to its very foundations and compel people everywhere to feel the impact of the kingdom of God in their midst.

The Pentecostal churches have their problems, as all churches do. Yet, in their teaching that everyone needs a personal Pentecost, they have not only led their people into that experience, they have made the Pentecostal churches throughout the world such a witnessing force that, while most other churches have been declining, they have been growing by leaps and bounds, so much so that reliable statisticians have described them as "the fastest-growing denomination in the world."

Jesus said very plainly that we needed to be empowered by the Holy Ghost before we could be His witnesses. If this was necessary for Peter and James and John and Mary and Martha, then how can any modern Christian expect to witness as they did unless with them he experiences a personal Pentecost?

Do we long to be Christ's witnesses? Do we feel powerless for such a task? Then let us pay heed to these words of our Lord: "Ye shall receive power after that the Holy Ghost is come upon you, and ye shall be witnesses unto me." We all need this power of Pentecost, if we are to be His effective witnesses. That power is available now, and with it we, like the Christians of the first century, can turn the world upside down. Ask! Seek! Knock!

Once More, Pentecost Means Power for Service

Pentecost does not mean an end of concern

about social problems and needs. On the contrary, it means being far more concerned about them!

How would a return of that New Testament level of life enable us to serve mankind?

Well, let us take one example of how it has in fact happened in one part of the world in relation to the crying problem of alcoholism.

We organize conferences in order to try to tackle the problem. We spend hours in committee hoping to find the best methods of dealing with it. Yet none of us could claim that we as a people are having tremendous success. In South America, however, where alcoholism was more widespread than in any other part of the world, the problem *is* being dealt with most satisfactorily.

How?

Let me quote from a South American Catholic priest: "For generations alcoholism has been one of the social plagues of Latin American countries. Its effects on the ill-fed population have been disastrous. Pentecostals have carried out a courageous campaign to wipe it out from individuals and from homes. Chilean Pentecostals have become sober and hard-working men who save their salaries, do not beat their wives, wear clean clothes, send their children to school. The laborers or the factory-workers most sought after by management are the Pentecostals. They are rated the best working men in the country." "Ye shall receive power after that the Holy Ghost is come upon you."

Those of us who are members of the older Christian denominations need this personal Pentecost. We need it for living; we need it for witnessing; we need it for serving the community. For, as we come more and more to know and to use this power, people will discover today, as they discovered in New Testament days, that we, the Church, possess what they most need. So powerfully will they feel the force of the moving of the mighty wind of God that they will return to the church of their fathers, there to be filled to overflowing with the power of God—power for living, for witnessing, for serving.

WHAT HAPPENED TO THE THREE HUNDRED AND EIGHTY?

Ian Macpherson

He appeared to more than five hundred brethren at one time. I Corinthians 15:6 (RSV)

The company of persons was in all about one hundred and twenty. Acts 1:15

Five hundred! One hundred and twenty! What a quick drop in numbers! What a swift thinning out of the ranks in something like thirty days! What a startling statistical reduction!

Of the more than half a thousand men who met the resurrected Master on the occasion to which Paul refers only about one-fifth were present in the Upper Room, "prostrate under the parted skies of Pentecost."

Why the numerical decline? What had happened to the three hundred and eighty?

It would be charitable to suppose that they were detained by the demands of duty. The supposition cannot, however, be sustained. Pentecost was the most popular of all the Hebrew religious festivals. Not even at the Passover did so many flock to the Holy City to keep the feast. Pentecost was *the* public holiday of the year, and nobody worked on a public holiday.

Where, then, *were* the three hundred and eighty?

Three reasons might be assigned for their absence from the Upper Room when the divine Spirit descended.

Take them one by one.

Perhaps they were not in the Upper Room because they thought they had gotten all God had for them when they saw the risen Christ.

That was a natural enough assumption. To have seen Jesus triumphant on the other side of the tomb must have been a truly tremendous experience. One might be forgiven for fancying that it was a terminal experience—that nothing could possibly be beyond it.

This is not so. You can see that from the account in Acts of Saul's encounter with the living Lord. Riding along the road to Damascus in the quivering heat of a Syrian noon, the young Pharisee is suddenly dazzled by a light brighter by far than that of the sun. Unhorsed, and lying in the dust, he looks up and beholds above him one whom he feels he knows and yet does not know. "Who art thou, Jehovah?" he cries. "I am Jesus," comes the answer.

Was that all God had for Saul? By no means. It was but the beginning of a relationship which it will take eternity to explore. "Go into the city," Jesus continues, "and it shall be told thee what thou must do." Saul does, and there he comes in touch with Ananias who tells him: "The Lord, even Jesus, who appeared unto thee in the way hath sent me that thou mightest be filled with the Holy Ghost."

There was something more for Saul than a meeting with the resurrected Christ. There was a mighty baptism in the Holy Spirit.

Or take another example. In his *Memoirs*

114

Charles Grandison Finney relates how one never-to-be-forgotten evening he went into a room in his house in Adams, N.Y., U.S.A. "It seemed," he records, "as if I met the Lord Jesus Christ face to face. It seemed to me a reality that He stood before me, and I fell down and poured out my soul to Him."

But that was not the full extent of Finney's experience. Walking in woods not far from his home some time later, he had a further encounter with the supernatural. "Without any expectation of it," he says, "without ever having the thought in my mind that there was such a thing for me, without any recollection that I had ever heard the thing mentioned by any person in the world, the Holy Spirit descended upon me in a manner that seemed to go through me, body and soul. It seemed like the very breath of God."

The three hundred and eighty may have been absent from the Upper Room on the day of Pentecost because they thought that, having seen the living Christ, they had gotten all that God had for them. They were in error. There was more.

Here are some wise words of Dr. Martyn Lloyd-Jones which are well worth quoting in this connection: "I am convinced that there are large numbers of Christian people who are quenching the Spirit unconsciously by denying these possibilities in their very understanding of the doctrine of the Spirit. There is nothing, I am convinced, that so quenches the Spirit as the teaching which identifies the baptism of the Holy Ghost with regeneration. So we say: 'Ah, well, I am already baptized with the Spirit. It happened when I was born again. It happened at my conversion. There is nothing for me to seek. I have gotten it all.' Gotten it all? Well, if you have gotten it all, I simply ask, 'In the name of God, why are you as you are?' No, it is wrong teaching."

Perhaps the three hundred and eighty were not in the Upper Room because they felt that the blessing was for the favored few but not for them.

Around our Lord, during the days of His flesh, there was a narrowing series of concentric social circles. In the outermost were the multitudes who waited upon His ministry; next came the seventy, to whom was delegated a special mission; closer still were the Twelve; and nearest of all the Three—Peter, James and John—who were admitted to the greatest and most intimate experiences of the Saviour's historic career.

Now, the three hundred and eighty did not belong to any inner circle. They were to some extent outsiders. Paul calls them "brethren," but gives us no further information as to their identity. The Eleven, we know, were in the Upper Room. There is no question about that. Maybe the three hundred and eighty considered themselves ineligible for the high privilege.

They were wrong. Pentecost is not for a meager minority. It is for all.

Years ago in a town in the north of England I used often to see a man, lean as a lath, pacing up and down the pavement of the principal thoroughfares, carrying sandwich-boards. If anybody seemed in need of a good meal, it was he. Gaunt, haggard, cadaverous, he strolled through the streets, advertising the most palatial restaurant in the place. "Come to the Ritz for the finest dinner in town," bawled his billboard. But always the banquet was for somebody else—never for himself!

There are Christians like that. Passionately, they believe that there is such a thing as a Spirit-filled life; they are quite sure, from their familiarity with Christian biography, that many in the past have undergone a thrilling baptism of power—John Wesley in London, Dwight L. Moody in New York, Oswald Chambers in Dunoon, and so on. But they cannot credit that the Whitsuntide experience is for them. They fancy it is merely for the favored few. But the promise is to "as many as the Lord our God shall call."

Perhaps the three hundred and eighty were not in the Upper Room because they had forgotten the direct command of Christ.

"Being assembled with the disciples, the risen Jesus commanded them that they should not depart from Jerusalem, but wait for the promise of the Father" (Acts 1:4).

All spiritual impoverishment results from failure to obey divine directions. "Wait!" says Jesus. We are so impatient, so activist. "The trouble," as William Booth put it, "is that God is not in a hurry, and I am." "Wait," says Jesus. All really effective action begins in a human passivity which is the prelude to divine activity. The three hundred and eighty had an appointment with God that fine May morning long ago, but they failed to keep it. The Holy Spirit did not descend on them where they were. He did not baptize them on the Galilean hills or on the shore of the Mediterranean, or wherever they happened to be. They were not in the home of Mrs. Mark, High Street, Jerusalem, and so they missed the mighty visitation. They were not there when the Church was born.

At this season of the year, when we commemorate the coming of the Comforter, let us

117

see to it that we are in the place of divine appointment, wherever that may be, our eyes uplifted, our hearts wide open, for

> *God's skies are full of Pentecosts,*
> *For you, for me, for all.*

Other books
you may want to read . . .

AMERICA'S GREAT REVIVALS
Here is the thrilling story of spiritual revival in the United States as led by Jonathan Edwards, D. L. Moody, Jeremiah C. Lanphier and Charles Finney. 75¢

CRISIS EXPERIENCES IN THE LIVES
OF NOTED CHRISTIANS
by V. Raymond Edman
Here are the personal testimonies of V. Raymond Edman, J. Hudson Taylor, Walter Wilson, Dwight Moody, William T. Nicholson (and others) telling of their crisis spiritual experience after conversion. 75¢

FATHER OF COMFORT
by Basilea Schlink
These short devotions for every day of the year are meant to teach us how to put our trust in the Father during all circumstances $1.25

HOW TO FIND FULNESS OF POWER
by R. A. Torrey
This book is written to show that there is a way to find abiding rest, joy, satisfaction, and power. 95¢